W9-COG-572

Illegal Immigration

Illegal Immigration

Other Books in the Current Controversies Series:

The Abortion Controversy
Alcoholism
Assisted Suicide
Capital Punishment
Censorship
Child Abuse
Computers and Society
Conserving the Environment
Crime
The Disabled
Drug Legalization
Drug Trafficking
Ethics
Europe
Family Violence
Free Speech
Garbage and Waste
Gay Rights
Guns and Violence
Hate Crimes
Hunger
Illegal Drugs
The Information Highway
Interventionism
Iraq
Marriage and Divorce
Medical Ethics
Mental Health
Minorities
Nationalism and Ethnic Conflict
Native American Rights
Police Brutality
Politicians and Ethics
Pollution
Prisons
Racism
Reproductive Technologies
The Rights of Animals
Sexual Harassment
Sexually Transmitted Diseases
Smoking
Suicide
Teen Addiction
Teen Pregnancy and Parenting
Urban Terrorism
Violence Against Women
Violence in the Media
Women in the Military
Youth Violence

Illegal Immigration

Helen Cothran, *Book Editor*

CURRENT CONTROVERSIES

Cover photo: © Joe Raedle/Newsmakers

Library of Congress Cataloging-in-Publication Data

Illegal immigration / Helen Cothran, book editor
p. cm. — (Current controversies)
Includes bibliographical references and index.
ISBN 0-7377-0684-8 (pbk. : alk. paper) — ISBN 0-7377-0685-6 (lib. : alk. paper)
1. Illegal aliens—United States. 2. Illegal aliens—Government policy—United States. 3. Emigration and immigration—United States. I. Cothran, Helen. II. Series.

JV6483 .I5 2001
304.873—dc21

2001023047
CIP

Printed in the U.S.A.

Contents

Foreword

By definition, controversies are "discussions of questions in which opposing opinions clash" (Webster's Twentieth Century Dictionary Unabridged). Few would deny that controversies are a pervasive part of the human condition and exist on virtually every level of human enterprise. Controversies transpire between individuals and among groups, within nations and between nations. Controversies supply the grist necessary for progress by providing challenges and challengers to the status quo. They also create atmospheres where strife and warfare can flourish. A world without controversies would be a peaceful world; but it also would be, by and large, static and prosaic.

The Series' Purpose

The purpose of the Current Controversies series is to explore many of the social, political, and economic controversies dominating the national and international scenes today. Titles selected for inclusion in the series are highly focused and specific. For example, from the larger category of criminal justice, Current Controversies deals with specific topics such as police brutality, gun control, white collar crime, and others. The debates in Current Controversies also are presented in a useful, timeless fashion. Articles and book excerpts included in each title are selected if they contribute valuable, long-range ideas to the overall debate. And wherever possible, current information is enhanced with historical documents and other relevant materials. Thus, while individual titles are current in focus, every effort is made to ensure that they will not become quickly outdated. Books in the Current Controversies series will remain important resources for librarians, teachers, and students for many years.

In addition to keeping the titles focused and specific, great care is taken in the editorial format of each book in the series. Book introductions and chapter prefaces are offered to provide background material for readers. Chapters are organized around several key questions that are answered with diverse opinions representing all points on the political spectrum. Materials in each chapter include opinions in which authors clearly disagree as well as alternative opinions in which authors may agree on a broader issue but disagree on the possible solutions. In this way, the content of each volume in Current Controversies mirrors the mosaic of opinions encountered in society. Readers will quickly realize that there are many viable answers to these complex issues. By questioning each author's conclusions, students and casual readers can begin to develop the critical thinking skills so important to evaluating opinionated material.

Current Controversies is also ideal for controlled research. Each anthology in the series is composed of primary sources taken from a wide gamut of informational categories including periodicals, newspapers, books, United States and foreign government documents, and the publications of private and public organizations. Readers will find factual support for reports, debates, and research papers covering all areas of important issues. In addition, an annotated table of contents, an index, a book and periodical bibliography, and a list of organizations to contact are included in each book to expedite further research.

Perhaps more than ever before in history, people are confronted with diverse and contradictory information. During the Persian Gulf War, for example, the public was not only treated to minute-to-minute coverage of the war, it was also inundated with critiques of the coverage and countless analyses of the factors motivating U.S. involvement. Being able to sort through the plethora of opinions accompanying today's major issues, and to draw one's own conclusions, can be a complicated and frustrating struggle. It is the editors' hope that Current Controversies will help readers with this struggle.

Greenhaven Press anthologies primarily consist of previously published material taken from a variety of sources, including periodicals, books, scholarly journals, newspapers, government documents, and position papers from private and public organizations. These original sources are often edited for length and to ensure their accessibility for a young adult audience. The anthology editors also change the original titles of these works in order to clearly present the main thesis of each viewpoint and to explicitly indicate the opinion presented in the viewpoint. These alterations are made in consideration of both the reading and comprehension levels of a young adult audience. Every effort is made to ensure that Greenhaven Press accurately reflects the original intent of the authors included in this anthology.

Introduction

On November 25, 1999, eleven Cubans drowned at sea on their way to the United States in search of a better life. There was only one survivor: a five-year-old boy named Elián González. Ordinarily, undocumented immigrants are quickly returned to their homelands. After Elián was rescued by the U.S. Coast Guard, however, his case became a heated custody battle and a divisive political issue.

On the one hand were relatives of the boy who were living in the United States as legal residents. Because Elián's mother died trying to bring him to Florida, they maintained, it was clear that she had wanted the boy to live in the United States. They argued that returning Elián to Communist-led Cuba was equivalent to taking away his freedom. When five-year-old Elián requested political asylum, many thought his relatives had pressured him to do so.

On the other hand, U.S. immigration law has traditionally granted parents the right to make asylum determinations for their children. Thus, the Immigration and Naturalization Service (INS)—at the request of Elián's father, who still resided in Cuba—decided to return the boy to his homeland. An appeals court later ruled that Elián should remain in the United States, but in June 2000, the U.S. Supreme Court overruled that decision and ordered the boy returned to Cuba to live with his father.

The Elián González case highlights many controversies: The United States' relationship with sending nations such as Cuba, INS asylum policies, and the political autonomy of children. By far the most complex issue it underscores, however, is the nature of national sovereignty. The United States has one of the most open borders in the world, taking in around 700,000 immigrants a year. It does not have an open border, however, and regulates who can come, from where, and in what numbers. Although the United States attempts to control who enters the nation, thousands of people a year from all over the world break U.S. immigration laws and enter illegally. The INS estimates that over five million illegal immigrants live in the United States. Some of those people—like Elián González—apply for political asylum in order to escape political persecution.

Immigration policy is designed to address two basic concerns: one, the well-being of people in other parts of the world who are fleeing oppression and poverty; and two, the well-being of the United States. Like any nation, the United States has elected to give priority to its own people. But the United States occupies a unique position: since its founding, it has been a symbol of freedom and justice in the world. As such, the United States has been a magnet for those fleeing oppression in their own countries.

Conflicts concerning immigration policies often arise when the welfare of U.S. citizens seems to take a back seat to the welfare of immigrants and refugees. Garrett Hardin, professor emeritus at the University of California,

Santa Barbara, uses a lifeboat analogy to illustrate this ethical problem. If the United States is pictured as the lifeboat—which has a finite carrying capacity—it must choose how many people to invite aboard. With relative safety, the United States can allow some specified number of people in. This option protects native-born citizens and legal immigrants, but dooms those denied entrance to possible death. Or, the United States can accept all who want to get in and exceed the carrying capacity of the boat. At that point, all passengers—including the immigrants recently allowed aboard—would die.

The journalist Bruce A. Ramsey agrees that the United States must not establish an open door immigration policy. He argues that no rich nation in the world allows open immigration because such an action would be catastrophic to that country's economy. He writes: "Just imagine it. Shiploads of boat people. Haitians, Dominicans, Jamaicans, Javans, Punjabis, Pathans, Yorubas. You could have people camped on school playgrounds, in city parks, along the streets, and in Shantytowns speaking strange languages." In consequence, he argues, "the minimum wage would be swept away, welfare swamped, food stamps shredded."

John Vinson, president of the American Immigration Control Foundation, an organization that advocates strict immigration controls, paints an even bleaker scene. He worries about immigration's impact on social cohesion. Americans, he contends, have two choices: "either reduce our current rate of immigration, which is now greater than at any time in the past, or witness the passing and death of America as waves of foreign people and cultures submerge our land." Pat Buchanan, a notable figure in American politics, concurs: "If America continues on its present course [of allowing so many immigrants in], it could rapidly become a country with no common language, no common culture, no common memory and no common identity."

Many opponents of open borders criticize U.S. asylum policies. John Tanton, in a testimony before the Senate Subcommittee on Immigration and Refugee Policy in October 1981, argued that "if amnesty is given to a class on the basis of their having broken the law [by coming to the United States illegally] . . . then it is by its very definition a reward for that criminal act." Those who oppose open borders contend that asylum opens the floodgates to illegal immigrants and threatens to swamp the lifeboat. Many believe that asylum is abused by refugees who leave their homelands for economic reasons, not political ones.

Not everyone accepts Hardin's lifeboat analogy, however, nor do they believe the doomsday predictions of immigrant opponents like Ramsey and Vinson. Advocates of open borders contend that national immigration policies privilege those already living in the country over those who desire to get in. By closing its borders to people, immigration advocates assert, the United States relegates them to poverty, persecution, even death. In other words, the United States has a moral obligation to allow as many people into the lifeboat as want aboard. Many people who are denied legal entrance will simply enter illegally, they add, and will live in the country as permanent, disenfranchised residents.

Dan Lacey, an author on employment-related subjects until his death in 1993, uses a table rather than a lifeboat analogy to argue for open borders. He writes, "there are mountains of evidence that there will never be too many people seated around the table . . . if America's borders were opened." He argues, "Immigrants don't consume prosperity, they create it." William B. Johnston, vice-president of special projects at the Hudson Institute, a non-partisan policy research organization, compares Los Angeles with Detroit in his argument for open borders. He writes: "There are very few immigrants in Detroit and overwhelming numbers of immigrants in Los Angeles. And yet Los Angeles is a much better place to find a job, and it has a much faster growing economy than that of Detroit." Immigrants provide a dynamic workforce that fosters production, immigrant proponents argue, and that helps the economy grow.

Many immigration advocates, believing that immigrants contribute vitality to American culture, disagree with analysts like Buchanan who claim that open immigration threatens social cohesion. Everett Carll Ladd, professor of political science at the University of Connecticut, maintains that "the immigration experience hasn't weakened or fundamentally altered the country. Rather, it has strengthened and renewed it." Ladd believes that American identity is not based on ethnicity but on an idea, a set of beliefs. According to Ladd, "immigrants say they came to the US seeking economic opportunity and freedom for themselves and their children." Every wave of immigrants, he claims, embraces that ideal, which strengthens, not undermines, social cohesion.

Considerations such as economic opportunity and political freedom make political asylum a highly charged issue. Elián González's case, for example, called into question many of the assumptions people hold about illegal immigrants and the countries from which they come. The little Cuban boy captured the hearts of many Americans who believed that he would be happier in the United States than in Cuba. But doubters wondered if Cuba was truly a worse place to live than the United States. Perhaps, they speculated, life is just different there, not necessarily better. Others wondered if the United States was obligated to help people like Elián, and if granting the boy political asylum would set a precedent for other refugee children to request asylum, perhaps causing a wave of fraudulent asylum requests.

To be sure, people of good will often argue heatedly about immigration questions raised by cases such as Elián's. Educators, politicians, and other experts debate many of the issues surrounding illegal immigration in the following chapters: Is Illegal Immigration a Serious Problem? Does Illegal Immigration Harm the United States? Does the United States Treat Illegal Immigrants Fairly? and, How Should the United States Respond to Illegal Immigration? Elián González is back in Cuba, but it is certain that other illegal immigrants, old and young, will cross the nation's borders hoping to find a better life in the United States.

Chapter 1

Is Illegal Immigration a Serious Problem?

Chapter Preface

David sat in the dark hold of the boat named *Believe in God*, fighting thirst and nausea. He and forty-three other Haitians were crossing the ocean toward the Bahamas where they planned to board another boat and head for Florida. But their dream of entering the United States illegally quickly receded in the face of misery and fear.

Between 6,000 to 12,000 Haitians enter the United States illegally every year, according to Michael Finkel, a journalist who traveled with David aboard the *Believe in God*. The U.S. Coast Guard estimates that thousands of other immigrants perish each year in the turbulent seas near the Bahamas. Like most immigrants, Haitians leave their country—the poorest in the Western hemisphere—in order to find work.

Illegal immigrants travel to the United States by sea, land, or air. Sea travel is especially perilous, but the journey by land also involves danger. Many illegal immigrants from Mexico, for example, drown in the Rio Grande River while trying to cross into Texas. Those crossing the rural areas of California and Arizona face treacherous mountains and deserts. In 1998, 145 illegal migrants died from dehydration in these desolate areas, according to the American Civil Liberties Union. In San Diego County, some immigrants die in wildfires ignited by their own campfires.

Entering the United States by air also involves hardship. Some illegal immigrants attempt to steal the passports of legal passengers and try to pass them off as their own. Immigration officials are rarely fooled by this tactic, however, and usually apprehend the illegal immigrants who then face detention—which can last many months—in prison-like conditions. Another strategy that illegal immigrants attempt is to leave their home countries legally, then destroy their papers on the plane or in the airport and apply for political asylum. Processing asylum cases takes a long time, however. Those waiting to have their cases heard often face detention. If their asylum claims are denied, illegal immigrants are deported to their home countries where they can face torture and death despite having left legally.

Although people who enter the United States illegally face many perils, many U.S. citizens and immigration experts find it difficult to sympathize with them. These immigration opponents believe that those crossing illegally know the risks and must suffer the consequences of their folly. Samuel Francis, a syndicated columnist, argues that illegal immigrants, having broken the law when entering the United States, continue to flout America's laws while living in the country. According to Francis, there are many organized criminal gangs made up of illegal immigrants as well as "unorganized common criminals who are immigrants and who regularly prey on American victims." Illegal immigrants are criminals, many analysts maintain, and do not deserve compassion.

Michael Finkel reports that David and the other Haitians aboard the *Believe in God* intended to find honest work in the United States, but no one will ever know whether they would have became laborers or criminals. *Believe in God* was stopped by the U.S. Coast Guard and all forty-four of its passengers returned to Haiti. The authors in the following chapter debate whether or not illegal immigration is a serious problem. Included in their debate is how illegal immigrants get to the United States and from where they come.

Illegal Immigration Is a Serious Problem

by Brent Ashabranner

About the author: *Brent Ashabranner writes books for young adults on social issues.*

Every morning at six o'clock Roberto leaves his shabby room in a Los Angeles boardinghouse and walks eight blocks to a street where mostly Hispanic men in work clothes have already begun to gather on the sidewalk. Like Roberto, they are illegal immigrants, and also like Roberto, they hope that a labor recruiter will come by and pick them for a day's work on a construction job. Hiring illegal aliens is against the law, but some employers are willing to take the risk because illegals will work for less pay and expect no job benefits beyond their daily pay.

With only a few years of elementary-school education, Roberto had never been able to find work in Hermosillo, Mexico, where he was born and grew up. He lived with his parents, who were very poor and who had eight other younger children. On his twenty-first birthday, Roberto decided to go to the United States. Some of his friends had gone already, and he had received a letter from one in Los Angeles who said there were jobs in that city. Roberto knew that he would never be approved as a regular immigrant, so he decided to cross the border illegally.

Roberto's mother gave him her blessing to leave Mexico; she also gave him a hundred dollars, all she could borrow from a money lender. Roberto went to Tijuana, a Mexican border city near San Diego, California. After a few days he located a "coyote," a person who guides or smuggles illegal aliens across the border. The coyote got him to San Diego, but Roberto had to give the man all of his money, keeping only enough for a bus ticket to Los Angeles.

For the past two years Roberto has begun almost every day standing on the same Los Angeles street hoping to be chosen for a job. He works two or three times a week and makes barely enough to live on, which he could not do in Mexico.

Chapter 1

Rina

Rina is twenty-six, a native of the Central American country of El Salvador. After her husband died of cancer, Rina was unable to make a living for her four children and herself. Finally, she left her children with her sister and started for the United States. She traveled through Guatemala and Mexico, sometimes by bus, sometimes begging rides on trucks. Often she walked all night, sleeping a few hours beside the road.

Her journey took more than three weeks, but at last she reached the city of Nogales on the border. Nogales, Mexico, and Nogales, Arizona, are sister cities, and it was not hard to find a way to slip into Nogales on the U.S. side. But it was not easy to elude the U.S. Border Patrol. Rina was caught five times as she crossed into Arizona. Each time she convinced the Border Patrol agents that she was Mexican, and after she signed the voluntary return form, they sent her back across the border. Had the Border Patrol known she was from El Salvador, they could not have returned her to Mexico; she would have been put in a detention camp for probable return to her own country.

When she had almost given up hope, a Mexican acquaintance who felt sorry for her gave Rina a school uniform to wear and a book to carry. She crossed the border once more and this time with her "disguise" escaped detection by the Border Patrol. Rina made her way to a Texas city and found work as a housecleaner and later as a live-in baby-sitter. Within a few months she was sending money back for her children and even beginning to save. Then one night she was robbed and beaten, her arm shattered. Now she is recovering in a Catholic shelter which does not ask whether a person is an illegal immigrant.

"Each time she convinced the Border Patrol agents that she was Mexican, and after she signed the voluntary return form, they sent her back across the border."

When her arm heals, Rina will try again to find work so that she can support her children in El Salvador.

Alex

Alex was born in Mexico City into a family of nine children. His father is a factory worker. After Alex graduated from middle school, he wanted to go to trade school, but the family had no money to send him, and he was unable to earn money for school fees. So when Alex was sixteen, he went to Texas with a friend, crossing the Rio Grande at night near Matamoras, the sister city of Brownsville, Texas. Alex hitched rides to the Texas city where his brother lives; his brother is a legal resident of the United States, but that does not help Alex. He is still an illegal alien.

With his brother's assistance, Alex goes to school. He is a good student and will soon graduate from high school. Alex wants to stay in the United States, but as an illegal alien his chances of finding a steady job are poor. Still, he refuses to give up hope.

Cyprian

Cyprian is a young West African taxi driver. He is a good driver, cheerful, polite, and without a single accident to blemish his record. He has learned the city quite well and can take his customers to their destinations quickly. The most unusual thing about Cyprian is that he is not driving a taxi in his native city of Lagos, Nigeria. Instead, he drives his cab through the somewhat complicated streets of Washington, D.C.

> ***"Thousands of people . . . come to the United States legally each year but do not leave when their [temporary] visas expire."***

Cyprian came to Washington four years ago to study at George Washington University. He had a passport and a student visa valid for two years. His government paid his expenses. At the end of two years Cyprian wanted to extend his study for another year, but his government said no. Even though his visa had expired and he was supposed to leave the country, Cyprian decided to stay in Washington. A friend gave him the taxi job, and he is taking night courses at George Washington. Cyprian knows that he is breaking the immigration law, but tries not to think about that. He likes America and has decided he wants to stay.

Illegal Aliens and Visa Abusers

Hundred of thousands of people like Roberto, Rina, and Alex come to the United States every year. They do not have a passport with an entry visa or any other legal border-crossing permit. They do not pass through an official port of entry as all persons who enter the country legally must do. In the language of the U.S. Immigration and Naturalization Service (INS), they are "undocumented." They are illegal aliens. Almost without exception, they are people who would have little chance of being approved as legal immigrants or would have to wait years for approval.

Thousands of people like Cyprian come to the United States legally each year but do not leave when their visas expire. They do not come on immigrant visas, but rather on temporary visas as tourists, students, or for business purposes. When their visas expire and they fail to leave the country, they become illegal aliens and are classified by the INS as "visa abusers." Visa abusers come from Africa, Asia, Europe, and every other part of the world.

The full dimensions of illegal immigration to the United States are hard to grasp because they involve countless stories of hardship and human need. But the cold, hard statistics of illegal immigration tell their own troubling story.

• An estimated 4 million illegal immigrants live in the United States today. This figure, as well as most of which follow, comes from the INS Statistics Division. Precise figures are impossible to obtain for the simple reason that illegal immigrants do not want to be counted.

• An estimated 300,000 illegal aliens settle permanently in the United States every year.

• The total number of illegal aliens entering the United States each year is much higher, between 1.5 million and 2.5 million. The majority are young single men. Most of these persons are called "sojourners." They come to do seasonal agricultural work or to visit family members living in the United States and then return home after a short stay. Many who come with the intention of staying permanently become discouraged and return home when they can't find work.

"An estimated 300,000 illegal aliens settle permanently in the United States every year."

• More than 30 percent of all illegal immigrants in the United States are Mexicans.

• Over 3.4 million "deportable aliens" were apprehended crossing U.S. land borders or landing on U.S. shores during the years 1992–1994. Over 95 percent of those apprehended were persons who illegally crossed the U.S.–Mexican border.

• Regardless of where or how they entered the United States, illegal aliens from 170 different countries were apprehended in 1994.

A Nation of Laws

Throughout its history the United States has received more immigrants from more countries than any other nation in the world. In recent years legal immigrants have totaled nearly 1 million annually. Over the centuries the United States has drawn richly from the cultural backgrounds of many immigrant groups—ideas, languages, customs, music, dance, food, dress—to forge a new culture, an American culture. We are truly a nation of immigrants.

But we are also a nation of laws. Americans who strongly support our national immigration program are troubled by the fact that millions of people enter, or try to enter, the United States illegally every year and that millions continue to break the law by staying here. In a *Washington Post* article entitled "Immigration: Making Americans," William J. Bennett is very positive about our legal immigration program. But in the article, Bennett, a former Secretary of Education, writes: "Illegal immigration is a very serious problem, and all Americans . . . are right to be upset and angry. Every sovereign nation has the right and the duty to control its borders."

Why is illegal immigration a serious problem?

The most obvious answer is that persons entering the country illegally and living here illegally show a disregard for the nation's laws. They may break no other laws once they are here; but they have broken the law by sneaking across the border, and they will remain lawbreakers simply by staying here. They will never be able to take part fully and responsibly in the life of the country because they do not belong here.

On a concrete level, numbers alone are at the heart of the problem, particularly their concentration in a few states.

According to INS statistics, 70 percent of all illegal aliens in the United States live in California, New York, Texas, Florida, and Illinois. Most illegal aliens are poor. Their high concentration in a few urban locations in those states causes problems of low-cost housing availability and strains health, educational, and other social and charitable services.

High Costs

The cost of fighting illegal immigration adds to an already overburdened national budget. The Border Patrol appropriation for 1994 was almost half a billion dollars and is certain to grow in future years. Illegal immigration has created a criminal industry in the manufacture and sale of fake Social Security cards, birth certificates, work permits, and other documents used to prove legal residence in the United States. The INS now spends over $300 million each year to combat document fraud, to enforce the law prohibiting employment of illegal immigrants, and to find and deport persons living illegally in the country.

Visa Abuse Is a Serious Problem

by Ashley Dunn

About the author: *Ashley Dunn writes for the* New York Times.

In the comfort of a KLM flight from Belfast, Francis and Theresa S. arrived in the United States in October 1994 as tourists. But they had no intention of returning to their home in Northern Ireland after their sightseeing in New York was over. They were coming to stay on as illegal immigrants.

Unlike the thousands of Mexicans and Central Americans clambering over the flood-lit fences of the southern border, the couple merely walked through an inspection booth at Kennedy International Airport. An immigration official, checking their passports and plane tickets, smiled and waved them in.

"It was that easy," said Francis, who along with his wife did not want to be fully identified for fear of being uncovered. "They just stamped our passports and that was it," he said as he sat in a bakery in Woodside, Queens, taking a break from moving into a new apartment with his wife.

No Deterrence for Visa Abuse

Slightly more than half of the nation's illegal immigrants, including the vast majority in the New York area, casually enter the country as tourists, students or business people, and then simply overstay their visas.

And although the Immigration and Naturalization Service (INS) spends millions to patrol the southern border, the agency virtually ignores those illegal immigrants who, like Francis and Theresa, have walked in through the nation's front door.

"There is absolutely no deterrence," said David Simcox, a senior fellow of the Center for Immigration Studies in Washington, which favors restrictions on immigration. "There isn't much there to stop anyone."

In fact, the INS has no specific programs aimed at seeking out and deporting the 150,000 visitors a year who end up illegally settling here. In 1994, only about 600 people were deported for overstaying their visas, out of 39,000 deportations.

An International Problem

The estimates on illegal immigrants come from an INS study that uses air passenger data, census surveys and immigration service statistics. While the numbers provide only a rough approximation, they point out in broad strokes the magnitude of the problem with illegal immigrants who overstayed their visits.

Of the four million illegal immigrants in this country, about two million first arrived as visitors. Unlike those who sneak across the border, those who enter as visitors come from a broad range of countries, including Italy, the Bahamas, Poland and the Philippines. Together, they constitute a far more diverse population than the public debate, focused on the border, tends to include.

In fact, outside of the border areas, Mexicans and Central Americans often make up only a small part of the illegal immigrant population.

More Visa Abusers than Border Crossers

Cecilia Munoz, a deputy vice president of the National Council of La Raza, a national Hispanic lobbying organization, said the Government's focus on the border has distorted the debate on how to control immigration, turning it instead into a blind bashing of Hispanics.

"Ninety-nine percent of enforcement efforts are directed at Latinos when, in fact, illegal immigration is far more diverse," she said. "The border does need to be controlled, but it is just half the problem."

In New York, which has the largest illegal immigrant population—529,000—after California, the biggest groups are from Italy, Ecuador and Poland. Mexicans are barely noticeable at just 2 percent of the state's illegal population.

Similarly, in New Jersey, with its population of 137,000 illegal immigrants, the three top groups are from Portugal, Poland and Italy.

Indeed, for illegal immigrants from the vast majority of countries, the most popular method for moving to the United States has been through overstaying a tourist or business visa.

Small Chance of Being Caught

Nuccio R., for instance, a 24-year-old illegal immigrant from Sicily, still marvels at the ease with which he came to the United States.

When he arrived at Kennedy four years ago, he simply collected his baggage and headed for his uncle's house in Brooklyn.

He had just graduated from high school and only planned to stay for a few months. But as he began to settle into life in America, he decided to stay for good. He has a full-time job in a relative's delicatessen, a car, a driver's license, credit cards and his own apartment in New Utrecht, near Bensonhurst.

"My life is pretty normal," he said. "Everybody knows I'm illegal. It's not a big deal."

And the chance of Nuccio ever being caught in this country by immigration authorities is virtually nil.

The immigration service's efforts to arrest illegal immigrants outside the border areas concentrate largely on workplace inspections.

Under the requirements of the 1986 Immigration Reform and Control Act, employers are required to check the immigration status of all employees, and are subject to penalties for hiring illegal immigrants. The theory behind the act was that the flow of illegal immigrants would slow as it became more difficult to find work.

> ***"Ninety-nine percent of enforcement efforts are directed at Latinos when, in fact, illegal immigration is far more diverse."***

But the law has proven easy to circumvent through the use of fraudulent documents or through work in the small shops and family businesses that ignore the law. And the immigration service also devotes few resources to enforce the law. In the New York area, 15 agents are responsible for investigating workplaces in 14 counties with over 12 million people.

Screening Out Potential Abusers

Chip Bogdanski, spokesman for the INS's New York district, said that, in many ways, the agency can do little more to screen visitors as they arrive. Of 22 million visitors yearly, only a tiny proportion, fewer than 1 percent, end up staying in the country, he said.

"That's not a bad ratio," Mr. Bogdanski said. "I mean we can't detain people arbitrarily and sit them down for four hours until they break. If their documents are in order, they have the money and they have reason to come here, what are you going to do?"

In theory, visitors who are likely to stay in the United States are screened out overseas by consular officials, who are responsible for issuing entry visas.

United States law requires that visa applicants be viewed as intending to immigrate permanently unless they can prove sufficiently strong ties, such as steady employment, family and property ownership, to their home country to insure return. A round-trip ticket is also required.

Nyda Novodvorsky Budig, spokeswoman for the State Department's Bureau of Consular Affairs, said that each year about a quarter of all visa applications are denied, although the rate can shoot well over 50 percent for some countries, including Bangladesh, Sierra Leone and Syria.

But even with the State Department's screening process, thousands still enter the country and stay on illegally. In the case of some countries, including Poland, Sierra Leone and Liberia, the overstay rate can shoot up to a quarter or more of all visitors, according to the immigration agency's estimates.

Visas have also proven to be fertile ground for a variety of smuggling schemes. In the last year, for example, Federal agents have discovered the growing use of temporary business visas by Russian illegal immigrants, who bank on the lesser scrutiny of visitors at ports of entry.

The problem with the screenings is that much of the consulate's decision is based on what applicants themselves present to their interviewers. Fraud is rampant and difficult to catch given the enormous number of applicants each year. And even such close ties to the homeland as children provide no guarantee that a visitor will return home.

A 50-year-old woman from India, who uses only the name Akka, left behind two young children when she came to the United States eight years ago as a tourist. She had no need to lie to a consular official, since leaving her children, who were 10 and 14, would be proof enough that she would return.

But instead, Akka found a job as a baby sitter and now believes she is close to winning her green card through the sponsorship of her employer.

Visa Waiver Program

Entering the country is even easier for residents of 22 countries in the so-called visa waiver program. All they need to come to the United States for up to 90 days is a round trip ticket.

The countries, largely from Western Europe, were selected for the program based on their low rate of visa denials.

But the list also contains some significant abusers of the system, including France, Sweden and Italy. According to INS statistics, from 1988 to 1992 about 5 to 10 percent of illegal immigrants who overstayed their visits came from visa waiver countries.

Some of the illegal visitors eventually come to the attention of immigration authorities when they change their immigration status in some way, usually to become permanent residents through marriage, work or the visa lottery.

But even then, few suffer any serious penalty because of the difficulty in proving that they intentionally lied in coming to this country. Deportations for overstaying a visit are virtually unheard of. For example, in 1993, just 29 Polish nationals, out of a total illegal population of 107,000, were deported for violating their nonimmigrant status.

> ***"Few [visa abusers] suffer any serious penalty because of the difficulty in proving that they intentionally lied in coming to this country."***

Many of the illegal visitors simply melt away into American society and bide their time until they can become legal residents, primarily through marriage, work or the visa lottery. Over just a four-year period surveyed by the immigration service's study, 246,000 visitors who overstayed their visits became legal residents. About 332,000 of those who overstayed their visits eventually returned home.

Francis, 26, and Theresa, 22, like many of those who want to stay, have pinned their hopes on the visa lottery and intend to apply every year until they win.

"If we got green cards, we'd be paying our taxes," Theresa said. "We only came to work and give our children a better future."

But even if they fail, they said, it is no problem for them to continue living as illegal immigrants. They both have jobs, he as a construction worker and she as a bakery worker, and have settled comfortably into their new home in Woodside, one of the centers of the Irish community in New York City.

"It's just like back home sometimes," Theresa said. "This has been like a working holiday for us."

Smugging of Chinese Illegal Immigrants Is a Serious Problem

by Anthony Kuhn

About the author: *Anthony Kuhn writes for the* Los Angeles Times.

Spurred by the potential for huge profits, traffickers are increasingly routing illegal Chinese immigrants through major U.S. airports, including Los Angeles International (LAX), according to U.S. immigration officials.

Smuggling by Air

The influx has strained airport employees, from immigration personnel working overtime to process the Chinese, to maintenance staff repairing plumbing clogged with documents that would-be immigrants try to flush down toilets.

In 1999, an average of 170 suspected illegal Chinese immigrants have been detained each month at LAX with fake or missing travel documents, officials said.

Rosemary Melville, deputy district director of the Immigration and Naturalization Service, or INS, in Los Angeles, said the agency was "marginally successful" at catching smugglers and their human cargo.

"But when you look at the numbers, you know we're not making a dent in getting at the source," she said in a telephone interview.

Snakeheads

In recent years, air travel between China and the U.S. has increased, reflecting expanding economic ties between the two countries. New airplanes and flight paths have allowed more nonstop flights, such as between Beijing and Detroit or Shanghai and Los Angeles.

Meanwhile, more aggressive policing of America's land and sea borders has prompted smugglers to switch to air routes.

"What we know about smuggling is that the smuggling adjusts and shifts very

Reprinted from "Human Smugglers Taking to the Air," by Anthony Kuhn, *Los Angeles Times*, July 4, 2000.

quickly," INS Commissioner Doris Meissner said at a news conference in Beijing on Monday.

Meissner, visiting China for the first time, is meeting with Chinese officials to share information and secure cooperation in combating human smuggling. Her delegation includes INS officials from Los Angeles, San Francisco, Seattle and other common entry points for illegal immigrants.

So far this year, the United States has repatriated about 2,700 Chinese who have come by air, and that number is expected to reach 4,000 by year's end, Meissner said. By comparison, 1,000 Chinese arriving by boat have been repatriated so far this year. No figures are available for the total number of suspected illegal Chinese immigrants arriving in the U.S.

Human smugglers, known in China as "snakeheads," now charge as much as $60,000 per person to get their customers into the U.S.

China-Towns

The INS delegation also will tour southeastern China's Fujian province, whose people continue a centuries-old tradition of migration that has helped populate China-towns around the world.

Fujianese account for 80% of the 10,000 illegal emigrants intercepted by Chinese authorities last year, according to official Chinese figures. The plight of Fujianese in failed smuggling attempts has captured worldwide attention, from the drowning of 10 passengers from the Golden Venture off New York in 1993, to the discovery of 58 dead Chinese in a truckload of tomatoes in Dover, England, in June 2000.

According to Jack Lin, the immigration agency's Beijing-based attache, would-be illegal immigrants commonly enter Chinese airports with a ticket for a non-U.S. destination, then swap boarding passes with a legitimate traveler bound for the United States. Others carry forged passports and visas, or real ones with altered photos.

> ***"Spurred by the potential for huge profits, traffickers are increasingly routing illegal Chinese immigrants through major U.S. airports."***

Lin said an average of one illegal passenger is caught on each of Northwest Airlines' direct flights from Beijing to Detroit. Others are caught transiting through Tokyo, London, or Bangkok, Thailand.

More disturbing to Chinese and U.S. officials are corrupt airport personnel. Diplomats say border police, airline staff and ground crew at Chinese airports have been bribed to allow illegal immigrants to get past checkpoints or to go directly to the tarmac and onto the plane.

When the illegal immigrants get to Los Angeles, they either try to get past U.S. immigration with fake documents or destroy their documents and apply for asylum.

INS officials must first confirm undocumented aliens' identities. Then, officials with knowledge of China's human rights conditions assess their asylum claims to see if they are legally entitled to remain.

Previously, most Chinese asylum applicants said that if they returned home, they would face punishment for violating their country's one-child policy. Now many claim to be members of the outlawed Falun Gong spiritual group. About 13% of Chinese applying for asylum in the U.S. are approved, Meissner said.

Illegal Immigration Through Canada Is a Serious Problem

by Mark Clayton

About the author: *Mark Clayton is a staff writer for the* Christian Science Monitor.

In early morning darkness, Safeyban Hashi set out on the first boat trip of his life—a 10-minute dash across the St. Lawrence River from Canada to the United States in an outboard driven by a "native man."

The price to smuggle Mr. Hashi, a young Somali, into the US on Nov. 7, 1996 was cheap: $370. Let off on the US shoreline, he was directed by the smuggler to walk up a path to a road, where a taxi waited to take him to a nearby bus station.

The Canadian Gateway

While some 1 million Mexicans illegally cross the US southern border each year, a smaller but fast-growing number of Asians, Europeans, and others are being smuggled across the lightly patrolled, but longer Canada–US border. Canada is becoming a major gateway for people being smuggled across the almost 4,000-mile border, US authorities say.

As many as 15,000 people annually are moved by smuggling rings through border "hot spots" near Vancouver, B.C., Niagara Falls, Ontario, and Cornwall, Ontario.

None is a hotter spot than the Cornwall stretch of the US–Canada border known as "Smugglers' Alley."

Here, in a tangle of islands, water, and provincial-state-international boundaries that provide perfect cover to smugglers, the St. Lawrence River meets the borders of Ontario, Quebec, New York State, and the Akwesasne Mohawk Indian reservation.

In this lucrative zone, cigarettes were once the contraband of choice. Now with lower cigarette taxes, it is liquor, weapons—and people.

Reprinted from "Refugees to Canada Slip to US on Mohawk Trail," by Mark Clayton, *Christian Science Monitor,* November 13, 1996. Permission conveyed through Copyright Clearance Center, Inc.

The Black Market

The smuggling of people is fast becoming the most lucrative part of the black-market business here, because fees to smuggle a single individual are usually much higher than the $370 charged Hashi for his short boat ride.

Last week Canadian and US authorities broke up a major international syndicate that charged up to $38,000 per person to smuggle people from China's Fujian Province, through Canada and then to the US. Cornwall was the final transit point used by the 13 arrested smugglers.

During 1995 and 1996, the ring had flown 30 to 40 people from Fujian Province each month—up to 400 a year, through Canada and into the US via Cornwall, says Randy Wilson, a detective in the Metro Toronto Police force. Yet many other rings go undetected, he says.

Richard Ashlaw, head of the six-man border patrol office at Massena, N.Y., transferred from the US–Mexican border near Del Rio, Texas, where a typical day involved rounding up scores or even hundreds of illegal immigrants from Mexico. He says he thought Cornwall region would be comparatively quiet.

"I was quite shocked at the amount of activity up here and the sophistication of the smugglers," he says. "There are not as many—but we're busy all the time." And he and staff are getting busier.

In 1996, for instance, the US Border Patrol caught 299 people sneaking into the US through the smugglers' alley region, compared with 189 caught in the region in fiscal year 1995, and 67 illegals in fiscal 1994.

Reservation's Unique Geography

Ed Duda, assistant chief for the border that runs across upstate New York, Vermont, and New Hampshire, says the number of people caught who are apparently funneled through the Akwesasne Reservation is rising, while there is a decrease in other areas he oversees.

"It's definitely shifting toward the reservation," Mr. Duda says. "It provides virtually unmolested passage because of the virtually unique geography and jurisdictional boundaries of that area."

> ***"A . . . fast-growing number of Asians, Europeans, and others are being smuggled across the lightly patrolled, but longer Canadian–US border."***

Lewis Mitchell, native police chief in St. Regis, Quebec, on the Mohawk reservation agrees there has been a jump in smuggling overall through the reserve since 1988. Only in 1995 and 1996 has the number of people smuggled through really surged, he says.

"Smugglers will bring liquor, illegal aliens, anything they can make money off of through the reserve," Chief Mitchell says.

"I've heard of them bringing loads of diapers. We work with the RCMP [Royal Canadian Mounted Police] and the [US] Border Patrol. But with our geography and all the waterways, we can't stop it or cover it all," Mitchell says.

Chapter 1

An Important Link

Several factors make the Indian reservation a key link in the smuggling chain. First, the reservation land lies across the international border with about 8,000 natives living on the Canadian side and 2,000 more on the US side. The reservation includes Cornwall Island, sitting strategically in the middle of the St. Lawrence River, between Cornwall and New York State.

A smuggler can leave Cornwall Island (Mohawk land) by boat, cross the river, drop a person off on the Canadian side of the reserve quite legally. Then the not-yet-illegal can walk by himself through the reservation, across the unmarked US border, and out the other side of the reservation.

> ***"Smugglers will bring liquor, illegal aliens, anything they can make money off of through the [Mohawk] reserve."***

Some illegals then take a taxi, have a limousine meet them, or walk south across Mohawk land and across the border, popping onto the highway from one of hundreds of back roads leading out of the reserve.

In Hashi's case, a friend dropped him on the east end of Cornwall Island, where he paid the smuggler, who then set out for the US side. Hashi took a $12 taxi ride to the bus station at Massena, N.Y., about 10 miles away.

He told the *Monitor* he missed an early morning bus, then slept overnight in a local motel. As he waited for the 9 a.m. bus to take him to Alexandria, Va., the next day, he was apprehended by US Border Patrol agent Jean-Pierre Plante. These days the border patrol checks every bus.

US and Canadian authorities avoid pointing fingers at the Mohawk reservation publicly, but privately say most smuggling flows through Mohawk land.

Although smuggling is not embraced by the vast majority of Mohawks living there, they and others say it is tolerated because a small but heavily armed group favors it and intimidates any who oppose them.

"It's only a small fraction of the native population—a few bad apples that are smuggling," says Mr. Plante. "But there are not enough men in the entire border patrol to cover all those little roads coming out of the reservation."

Yet neither the US nor Canadian federal government has an appetite for the sort of tough fight that would be needed to close smugglers' alley.

The Oka 'Incident'

A 1990 land dispute led to a gun battle in Oka, Quebec, on the nearby Khanawake reservation, which left one Quebec policeman dead. Since then, Canadian authorities have mostly left the Mohawks to govern themselves.

US authorities say they go on the reservations, but do not do so in any systematic way. Large signs along the highway leading through the Akwesasne reserve say: "No F.B.I., No I.R.S." while nearby banners portray native warriors toting automatic weapons.

Repeated phone calls to Mohawk authorities went unreturned. Vaughn Phillips, a Mohawk chief handling the justice portfolio for the reservation, did not return repeated phone calls.

Chief Mitchell of the Akwesasne police force says smuggling organizations, like the Chinese ring recently unearthed, are responsible for the flow of people coming into the reservation.

"These organizations come from all over Canada and the US" to smuggle people through, he says. "We don't ignore it if we come across it. But smuggling is not our mandate. It's a federal mandate."

How It Impacts a Local Community

Across the river in Cornwall, Ontario, a blue-collar town of 47,000 people, Mayor Ron Martelle says smuggling subtly undermines his community by introducing violent criminals, mostly unseen, into the community.

And when it pops into view it can be ugly, as happened last month when a boatload of people being smuggled across the St. Lawrence capsized and one woman from Pakistan drowned.

"Washington and Ottawa do not have the courage to address this situation, because in their lack of wisdom they feel it is politically incorrect to go onto that reserve and fix the situation," Mr. Martelle says. "The law is the law. But they don't want another Oka."

American border authorities say they have a close working relationship with Canadian law enforcement, but they complain that Canadian law makes it easy for travelers from some countries to arrive in Canada with little or no documentation and claim refugee status.

"Canadian law makes it easy for travelers from some countries to arrive in Canada with little or no documentation and claim refugee status."

As the wheels of the refugee review process grind, the "refugees" make their plans to be smuggled into the US—as in the case of the Chinese from Fujian Province.

Police say the "refugees" were told to request asylum immediately. Days later, the "refugees" were on their way over the border through smugglers' alley.

In Hashi's case, he made his way to Canada several years ago. He only recently decided to head for the US, shortly after a Canadian refugee board turned down his plea for asylum. He was set to be deported back to Mogadishu, Somalia.

Hashi's Story

"I didn't have any papers when I came to Canada, and now they said 'no' to me," says Hashi, standing dejectedly at the same bus station where he was caught that morning.

Canadian authorities confirm Hashi's refugee status was recently turned down. But Canada will not permit United States authorities to return Hashi because, like so many others, he had violated the terms of his refugee status when he crossed the border. He is a US problem now.

Because Hashi has no criminal record in Canada, Ashlaw and his fellow patrolmen decided he poses no threat to the US. There is no room for him in detention unless he is a criminal, Ashlaw explains.

Set to board the bus to Alexandria, Va., where he has relatives living legally in the United States, Hashi is told to report to an immigration officer every 30 days until his deportation hearing.

"I hope that I will be able to find a place in the United States," he says, standing at the steps of the bus, a navy-blue nylon blazer shielding him from the cold November wind. "I hope that I can stay here."

Illegal Immigration from Mexico Is a Serious Problem

by Debra J. Saunders

About the author: *Debra J. Saunders is a columnist for the* San Francisco Chronicle.

The American-Mexican border fence in Tecate, a truck stop of a town some 33 miles east of San Diego, California, doesn't look like a fence in many spots. In some places, the metal sections are gone. Lonely rods, with nothing but air between them, mark where a fence used to be. Not that these gaps make much of a difference. At the outskirts of the much larger, adjacent town of Tecate, Mexico, the fence ends.

A Porous Border

I drove past homes guarded by barbed-wire and barking dogs to the end of the fence with a small group of observers on Wednesday afternoon. There, we saw a man with a walkie-talkie—probably a "coyote," or paid human smuggler—preparing to lead groups of would-be immigrants across the great divide. A turn of the head revealed another man, apparently in the same business.

A cough was heard from the bushes. In minutes, a coyote led four hopefuls, tramping single-file, through the trash-infested wasteland, where wrappers clung to every bush. A companion noticed a syringe by his feet. The landscape was scarred from fires.

On Tuesday, at dusk, standing on the elevated walkway at the busy San Ysidro–Tijuana border, you could see a cluster of men waiting under a Tijuana billboard for their chance to slip into the promised land. They were not subtle. Why should they be? If they are caught, there generally is no penalty. They'll simply get a free ride back to Mexico.

Most of these illegal immigrants are probably looking for work. Some may be

Reprinted from "US–Mexico Border Still Far Too Porous," by Debra J. Saunders, *North County Times*, January 22, 1996. Reprinted with permission from the author.

in search of vital medical benefits not available to them in their own country. Or welfare—which offers more security than they can expect to find in their own back yard. Figure that most of these economic refugees are good people.

Threats and Destruction

But even good people can be responsible for refuse and destruction. And the bad people—the coyotes they hire to get them across—are a menace. The *Alpine Sun* reported in September of 1995 that in the Highway 94 corridor near the border in San Diego County, there had been 73 fires so far that year—involving more than 11,000 acres—which officials attributed to "illegal border activity."

Ask Karl Saunders—no relation, although he's cantankerous enough to pass for one (only the stubborn remain in Tecate, U.S.A.). Saunders lives on a small ranch close to the border with his dog, three horses, a barn, and an outhouse. He can point to blackened swaths of earth where fires were set throughout August—by coyotes, he believes, who want to kill him because of his frequent calls to the U.S. Border Patrol. "I'm supposed to get scared and leave," he noted.

"In the . . . corridor near the border, there had been 73 fires so far [in 1995]—involving more than 11,000 acres—which officials attributed to 'illegal border activity.'"

Saunders is glad for Operation Gatekeeper—the Clinton administration initiative to step up border patrols. Not of the same mind are immigration boosters, who charge that the border is becoming too militarized. To the news that Border Patrol agents working the Canadian border had arrived at the California and Arizona borders this week, as per President Bill Clinton's directive, Jorge Bustamante of the Northern Frontier Association in Tijuana complained, "This is a hostile move against Mexico."

Yeah, sure. Americans trying to protect their homes are being hostile to Mexico. Tell us another one.

Immigration Opponents Ignore the Economic Contributions of Illegal Immigrants

by Thomas Elias

About the author: *Thomas Elias is a columnist with* Southern California Focus.

No one questions whether immigrants—both legal and illegal—cost money in the short term.

Many of them draw survival-level stipends from the federal government, their children must be educated in public schools, some get publicly funded health services and the criminals among them must be prosecuted and kept in prison.

But the emphasis these short-term costs get from politicians like California Gov. Pete Wilson and from popular initiatives like California's Proposition 187[1] can make it easy to overlook the long-term benefits of immigration.

Immigrants Are Profitable

What are those benefits? Hundreds of new businesses joining the tax base, cheap labor for use by many contractors and homeowners, and hundreds of millions of tax dollars raised over the many decades the immigrants and their children will live in California.

Those benefits, often ignored in California, are the increasing focus of many politicians outside California and they form the basis of a unique new study from the Tomas Rivera Center, a Los Angeles–based Latino-oriented think tank.

It concludes the answer is yes, immigrants are profitable. One example: Educating one immigrant child in California costs an average of $62,600, but that

1. Proposition 187 sought to deny educational and medical benefits to the children of illegal immigrants. The proposition passed in 1994, but was later overturned by a mediator in 2000.

Reprinted from "Consider the Long-Term Benefits of Immigration," by Thomas Elias, *North County Times,* August 2, 1996. Reprinted with permission from the author.

immigrant will eventually pay $89,437 in funds used for education via state income and sales taxes over a 40-year employment life.

The study adds that when costs and taxes paid for all education and social service programs are added up, legal immigrants produce an average net profit of $24,943 for the state over their lifetimes. Even illegal immigrants are profitable: Their average surplus over 40 years of employment is $7,890.

Some Politicians Distort Negative Impact

Those findings conflict with an early-'90s study by Rice University Professor Donald Huddle, who concluded immigrants of all types are a drain on American society.

His findings fueled much of the drive for Proposition 187, which sought to deprive illegal aliens of virtually all public education and other government services. That initiative, passed during the Republican landslide of 1994, in turn spurred moves by Californians in Congress to take benefits not only from illegals, but also from legal immigrants.

> ***"Illegal immigrants are profitable: Their average surplus over 40 years of employment is $7,890."***

But even some Republicans buy into the logic of the Rivera center study and see the proposed new federal anti-immigrant laws as shortsighted.

New York Mayor Rudolph Giuliani, whose city is by far the largest immigrant center outside California, is one. He argues that any measure letting states exclude immigrant children from schools—even if it's just children of illegals—would devastate cities like his by forcing thousands of school-age youngsters into street gangs.

But even without that reasoning, the Rivera center figures make it clear that while the anti-immigrant tide may be politically expedient, it is surely shortsighted.

Politicians Exaggerate the Problem of Illegal Immigration

by Raymond G. Aragon

About the author: *Raymond G. Aragon is president of the San Diego La Raza Lawyers Association.*

The debate on the treatment of undocumented Mexican immigrants has hit a fever pitch, in the wake of the April 1, 1996 videotaped freeway beating outside Los Angeles [during which two Riverside County sheriff's deputies beat illegal immigrants after a car chase], and the April 6, 1996 fatal crash near Temecula [in which several illegal immigrants died after they tried to flee authorities].

Serfdom

It has helped focus attention on the fact that we as Californians have become increasingly split about the role of undocumented Mexican workers in our society, and intolerant about them as people. Immigrants are enticed to come play a key role in our reliant economy, but are assigned serfdom status immediately upon arrival.

Employers and consumers alike welcome this labor force with open arms, to clean our homes and hotel rooms, till our soil and wash dishes at our favorite eateries.

Most economists agree that immigrants are an integral part of these labor-intensive, minimum-wage trades and that they probably contribute more than they receive.

But just as there are those who rejoice in the benefits from members of this labor force, there are others who decry their presence, claiming that they steal jobs or only come to sponge off welfare or medicare.

Reprinted from "It's Time to Contain the Intolerance," by Raymond G. Aragon, *San Diego Union-Tribune,* April 12, 1996. Reprinted with permission from the author.

Demagogues

Interestingly, there is a third group, which simultaneously occupies both positions. It is generally comprised of politicians pandering for nativist votes, such as the Pete Wilsons [who tried to get the Republican nomination for the presidency] and Michael Huffingtons [who ran against Diane Feinstein for the U.S. Senate] of the 1994 campaign season.

The members of this group deliver speeches blasting the immigrant invasion, often with the border fence as a backdrop, and then return home for supper prepared by their personal cadre of undocumented housekeepers. This third element creates the most mischief, since it has the most influence on public opinion.

Regardless of how these segments feel or what they say, undocumented workers are a cultural fact of life in our region, located, as it is, on the edge of the underdeveloped Third World. The situation is not likely to change as we enter the next millennium. The debate will continue as to the number of immigrant workers needed and how they should enter. There should be no debate, however, as to how they are treated once they are here.

Immigrant Bashers

The trend in recent years has been to make American life more and more difficult for those who enter illegally. Competition has intensified, among immigrant bashers, as to which group can craft the most inhumane legislation or policy.

California's Proposition 187 was designed to take away health and educational benefits, the idea being that once immigrants are refused service at medical clinics and elementary schools, they would grab their kids and catch the next Greyhound south to their homeland.

The San Diego Union-Tribune even suggested that the victims of the televised beatings and others who ride this modern-day underground railroad, should be legally barred from filing civil suits in brutality cases. The message here is that would-be immigrants should stay in Mexico, since the legal system will provide no civil remedies when they are victimized.

Hatemongers

They would thereby be entitled to lower social status than livestock. This would, no doubt, create a grant of full civil immunity to hatemongers, who would rape, maim or even murder undocumented Mexicans. But why stop there? Why not remove their protection from criminal statutes, as well?

The so-called backlash against the victims of the April 1 beatings has been utterly despicable. No measure of vitriolic expression has been spared on the victims. Critics don't much care that blame for the chase may rest entirely with the driver.

"If they dare to enter illegally, they deserve what they get," or so the argument goes. Barely a whisper is heard about Riverside County Sheriff's

Deputy Tracy Watson, who is seen clubbing his compliant arrestee like a batter swinging at a fastball.

As the 1996 election season nears, we can expect the rhetoric and demagoguery to harden. During convention week in August 1996, there may well be more press conferences and speeches delivered from the border fence than from the podium in the Convention Center.

Although Gov. Pete Wilson may have stumbled on this issue during his doomed presidential race, most notably with his infamous anti-immigrant speech from the Statue of Liberty, presidential hopeful Pat Buchanan is hell-bent on keeping his flame alive.

Racial Scapegoating

With all the grumbling by the voices of hate and intolerance, we should never forget how easily racial scapegoating can get out of control. Angry words of intolerance toward foreigners can easily lead to violent action.

Such action can quickly escalate from isolated, violent clashes to societal-sanctioned racism. This is the lesson not just of far-off places like Dachau, Germany [site of Holocaust prison camp], but also of nearby Manzanar, site of a Japanese internment camp during World War II. No society is immune from the scourge of extremism.

Californians need to step back from the emotions of the moment and contemplate what kind of people we are. Do we sincerely ascribe to the protection of basic human rights contained in the Declaration of Independence and the Constitution, such as the guarantee of equal protection under the laws? Or will we choose to be indifferent to the forces of darkness and this form of modern day serfdom, where Mexican laborers are afforded no more dignity than ranch animals?

"It is time for all people . . . to speak out against this atmosphere of intolerance which has resulted in the demonization of Mexican immigrants."

It is time for all people, particularly our political and spiritual leaders, to speak out against this atmosphere of intolerance which has resulted in the demonization of Mexican immigrants and incites others to blame the victim when violent injustices occur.

There should also be a demand for full accountability for the April 1 televised beatings and the convening of a statewide or national conference to call for an end to the violence against undocumented, as well as documented, Mexicans and Latinos.

Illegal Immigrants Can Make Positive Contributions to Society

by Marlene Peralta

About the author: *Marlene Peralta is a writer for* New Youth Connections.

I have many friends who are living in this country without legal documentation. Most of them are doing very well in school and have big dreams.

My friend Maria (not her real name) and I came to this country in the same year, 1995. She came from Mexico, I came from the Dominican Republic.

When we met each other, she was a girl full of hopes. Her goal was to go to college and become a teacher. I didn't know she was illegal, so I thought her goals were going to be easy to achieve because she is an excellent student and earns good grades in school.

I Want the Best for My Friends—Even If They Are Illegal

But being illegal makes it harder for Maria to pay for college (she can't receive financial aid), and it will make it even tougher if she does graduate and goes to look for a job as a teacher.

Right now she is studying at a community college because it is the only school she can afford, and she does not know if she will have enough money to continue.

I know the issues around illegal immigration are complicated.

But when I see my friends struggling simply because they do not have legal papers, and when I see many of their dreams banished, it doesn't seem fair. When I think about it that way, the only difference between legal and illegal is that some have the legal papers, and others do not.

How can we solve this problem? It is a hard question to answer.

From my own experience as a legal immigrant, I don't believe people always come here for the best reasons, or know what they're getting into before they come.

In my country, the Dominican Republic, people who have lived in the United States return and tell everybody that the United States is the best place because you can find money on the streets, the clothes are cheap, so is the food, and just about everything is wonderful.

Before I came to this country, I thought that New York was a paradise.

But once I came here, I saw that there are a lot of racial problems, everything is not cheap, and many immigrants, both legal and illegal, face a difficult life.

As proof, you just need to look around and see that many people who were professionals in their countries, like doctors and teachers, work as dishwashers or as guards or in factories here.

Some Immigrants Would Be Better Off at Home

I think it would be better if some people stayed in the countries they live in; to make this more likely to happen, I think that the United States should provide money to foreign countries to help create jobs there.

I know that it is hard for the United States to help the entire world, but maybe we need to help the countries that have the greatest number of people who come to this country illegally, because I think it is one way to stop them from coming.

But I also think it is foolish to think that that will stop the flow of illegal immigrants, or that cutting off education or health care will stop them, either. It won't.

> ***"If illegal children get an education and adults have decent jobs, it's good for them, but it's also good for the country."***

As I already said, they don't know what this country is like, anyway, so they won't know if conditions for illegal immigrants become even worse. They just want to reach their American dream, no matter what they face.

So I think the government should provide the basic benefits to illegal immigrants, such as education, emergency health care and job protection.

It is true that some illegal immigrants commit crimes, sell drugs. And I think that these people should be deported because they are showing that they want everything easy.

They are not doing anything productive for the country, so there is no reason to keep them here.

We Should Help *All* Immigrants to a Better Future

But the government should not make life even worse for people who are already here illegally and are working hard.

If illegal children get an education and adults have decent jobs, it's good for them, but it's also good for the country, because they will work and improve the economy and their kids will do well in the future.

I think many people in the United States have so many fears of illegal immigrants not because they're so bad for the country, but because they're an easy scapegoat for people who aren't succeeding on their own.

They think illegal people are going to take their jobs and achieve positions of power.

Immigrants Built America

Most of my friends who are here illegally *are* capable and I think they should have a good future and contribute to this country. But because they do not have the legal papers, they don't have as much of a chance.

They are people who came here to work hard to achieve their goals.

When I hear stories about people like Jinan, who escaped to America to avoid persecution for his religious beliefs in China, I think the United States is unfair.

I know that he came illegally and that he doesn't have the same rights as a citizen or a resident.

But many people like Jinan risk their lives to get their dreams. I think that we have to remember that these people work hard and sacrifice. They take jobs other people don't want, so they should have the right to an education and a chance to succeed.

After all, it was immigrants who built America.

Chapter 2

Does Illegal Immigration Harm the United States?

Chapter Preface

In 1994, Californians voted in favor of Proposition 187, which barred illegal immigrants from receiving publicly funded education, social services and health care. The proposition also required that local law enforcement authorities, school administrators, social and health care workers report anyone they suspected of being in the country illegally.

Proposition 187 immediately became a divisive political issue. The law's most visible proponent, California governor Pete Wilson, got re-elected due in least in part to his stance on Proposition 187. Students in California's colleges protested the proposition, calling it mean-spirited and unfair. Health workers and educators protested the new role thrust upon them as informants. Indeed, the proposition highlighted the deep divide that separates those who believe that illegal immigration harms the United States and those who believe it does not.

The argument made by the supporters of Proposition 187 was based on the assumption that illegal immigrants abuse publicly funded services, thereby costing taxpayers money. Proponents argued that the children of illegal immigrants attend public schools at taxpayer's expense and go on welfare more often than the native born do, and point to data collected by the federal government to support their claim. The federal General Accounting Office found that "new immigrants use government assistance substantially more than the native born," according to Georgie Anne Geyer, a syndicated columnist. Those worried about illegal immigration also asserted that illegal immigrants cost California hospitals millions of dollars a year. Since public hospitals are required to accept all patients, they contended, hospitals have had to cover the medical costs of illegal immigrants, who have no health insurance and often lack money. The politicians who supported Proposition 187 and the Californians who voted for it believed that it was wrong to have to pay for services used by people who did not pay into them.

On the other hand, opponents of Proposition 187 contended that it inhumanely denied assistance to people in need. They argued that Mexican nationals and other persons of color would bear the consequences of the new law because skin color would be the criteria that teachers or nurses would apply in deciding who might be an illegal immigrant. The *St. Anthony Messenger*, a Catholic publication, argued that such a proposition "legitimates ethnic hatred and unleashes witch hunts." In any case, opponents felt it was inappropriate to ask teachers, social and health care workers to be informers against the people they were trained to help. Finally, many analysts simply disagree with the assumption that illegal immigrants use up public funds at a higher rate than they replace them. To the contrary, illegal immigrants pay more in taxes than they use in publicly funded services, they contended.

Proposition 187 was overturned in 2000 by a mediator who argued that the law was unconstitutional. Supporters of the bill will likely push for further restrictions on illegal immigration, however, and many teachers, nurses, and students will certainly oppose them. At the heart of the issue is disagreement about the consequences of illegal immigration. The authors in the following chapter debate whether or not illegal immigration harms the United States.

Illegal Immigration Adds to the Strain on Social Services

by Joseph E. Fallon

About the author: *Joseph E. Fallon researches ethnic and racial issues.*

During the past thirty-two years, Congress has enacted laws on immigration, citizenship, and territorial powers which are deconstructing the United States as both a "European" nation and a federal polity.

For nearly two hundred years after its independence from Great Britain in 1783, the United States was demographically a "European" nation with never less than 81 percent of the population being of European, and overwhelmingly Northern European, ancestry. As recently as 1950, European-Americans still constituted 90 percent of the total population of the United States.

The Changed Pattern of Immigration

But all this has changed under the continuing impact of the 1965 Immigration and Naturalization Act Amendments. The Congressional sponsors of this legislation publicly and repeatedly told the citizens of the United States it: (1) would not increase the annual levels of immigration, (2) would not lower the standards for admission, (3) would not redirect immigration away from Europe, and (4) would not alter the demographic make-up of the United States.

For example, Senator Robert Kennedy declared "the new immigration act would not have any significant effect on the ethnic composition of the U.S." His brother, Senator Edward Kennedy, floor manager of the bill in the Senate, asserted that "This bill is not concerned with increasing immigration to this country, nor will it lower any of the high standards we apply in selection of immigrants." And Representative Emanuel Celler, the dean of the House in 1965 and a Congressional opponent of U.S. immigration policy since 1924, insisted "the effect of the bill would be 'quite insignificant' on U.S. population" and "that the

Excerpted from "The Deconstruction of America," by Joseph E. Fallon, *Journal of Social, Political, and Economic Studies,* Winter 1997.

bill would not let in 'great numbers of immigrants from anywhere,' including Africa and Asia."

What the Senators and the Congressman emphatically proclaimed as truth proved to be totally untrue. Between 1968, the year when the 1965 immigration law fully took effect, and 1996, the annual level of legal immigration skyrocketed from approximately 300,000 to nearly one million.

During the 147 years between 1820 and 1967, of the 44 million immigrants legally admitted to the United States 80 percent came from Europe while another 9 percent came from Canada. As a result of the 1965 immigration act, of the more than 19 million immigrants legally admitted to the United States in the 28 years between 1968 and 1996 approximately 83 percent came from somewhere other than Europe or Canada. Asia and the Pacific islands accounted for more than six million or 34 percent of the total; Latin America and the Caribbean islands accounted for almost nine million or 46 percent, and Africa accounted for nearly half a million or about 3 percent.

During the last 28 years, immigration from Europe totaled less than 3 million or barely 15 percent of all legal immigration while immigration from Canada amounted to less than half a million or less than 3 percent of the total. This decline from the 1820–1967 levels is more pronounced than these statistics reveal. While immigration from Asia means ethnic Asian immigrants, and immigration from Latin America means, with the exception of Brazil and Haiti, "ethnic" Hispanic immigrants, immigration from Europe and Canada does not mean ethnic European immigrants. Africans, Asians, and Latin Americans are able to immigrate to various European countries, as well as to Canada, then remigrate to the United States under the quotas for those countries.

"Five million illegal aliens have already permanently settled in the United States and . . . this population is increasing by an additional 300,000 each year."

Illegal Immigrants from Developing Nations

This decline in European immigration is even more dramatic when you include illegal immigration. The Immigration and Naturalization Service conservatively estimates that five million illegal aliens have already permanently settled in the United States and that this population is increasing by an additional 300,000 each year. Illegal immigration, like legal immigration, is monopolized by the Third World. As of 1996, of the 2,684,892 illegal aliens granted amnesty by the 1986 Immigration Reform and Control Act (IRCA) more than 98 percent, 2,642,921, came from the Third World—i.e., Africa, Asia and the Pacific islands, and Latin America and the Caribbean islands.

Of the 41,775 illegal aliens amnestied between 1989 and 1996 and identified as having come from Europe, Canada, Australia, and New Zealand, it is highly probable that, just as in the case of legal immigration, many may have been Third World aliens who had previously immigrated to those countries before then illegally entering the United States.

The single largest source of both legal and illegal immigration to the United States is Mexico. Between 1989 and 1996, Mexico's share of legal immigration was 37 percent, 44 percent, 52 percent, 22 percent, 14 percent, 14 percent, 13 percent, and 18 percent, respectively. During those seven years, Mexico's share of all illegal aliens amnestied by the Immigration Reform and Control Act (IRCA) was 71 percent, 71 percent, 80 percent, 75 percent, 72 percent, 73 percent, 70 percent, and 78 percent, respectively. According to the Immigration and Naturalization Service, Mexicans represent 54 percent of the five million illegal aliens permanently residing in the United States.

"The magnet attracting . . . [immigrants], both legal and illegal, is the welfare state and its extensive financial benefits."

A September 15, 1996 poll conducted by the *Los Angeles Times* revealed that half of all Mexicans have a family member living in the United States and 20 percent of Mexicans (18 million people) said they too were likely to migrate to the United States looking for better paying jobs within the next twelve months.

India, however, is a potential rival to Mexico's position as the single largest source of immigrants to the United States. The June 1995 "International Gallup Poll Report: People's Satisfaction with Their Lives and Government" discovered that 7 percent of the population of India—65 million people—would like to immigrate to the United States.

The Welfare Magnet

According to the Census Bureau, the foreign-born population in the United States as of 1996 numbered approximately 25 million. Of this number—which is larger than the population of 49 of the 50 States—over 61 percent had arrived in the last 15 years, and more than 25 percent had arrived since 1990. In addition, 20 percent were illegal aliens and over 66 percent had not become U.S. citizens.

The magnet attracting such immigration, both legal and illegal, is the welfare state and its extensive financial benefits which Congress had, up to the time of the enactment of the Welfare Reform Act of 1996, made available to Third World immigrants. Publications overseas—such as What You Need to Know About Life in America sold in Taiwan and Hong Kong—and in the United States—such as the Chinese language *World Journal*—provide Third World immigrants with information on how they can obtain these benefits.

In lobbying against proposed legislative reforms to reduce welfare eligibility for immigrants, the Organization of Chinese Americans admitted that if welfare benefits were not available many Chinese-Americans would not sponsor their overseas family members for admittance to the United States.

Tax Exempt Subsidies for Immigrant Organizations

Judging by their actions, the conviction that Third World immigrants come to the United States because of its generous welfare system is apparently shared by a number of other advocates of Third World immigration. Billionaire George Soros, an opponent of immigration reform, has pledged $50 million to assist immigrants who lose their benefits under the Welfare Reform Act of 1996.

In January 1997, the first installment of nearly $12 million was distributed among twenty-two pro–Third World immigration groups, including the Catholic Legal Immigration Network ($3 million), the Fund for New Citizens ($2.5 million), the National Council of La Raza ($1 million), and the National Immigration Law Center ($1 million). This money will not be used for job training or job placement. Instead, it will be employed to expedite the naturalization of immigrants so that as U S. citizens they can continue to receive their welfare benefits.

A further attraction for Third World immigrants is the relative ease with which these benefits can be fraudulently obtained. [The U.S. Department of Justice] reports that the "INS does not act against aliens who pay bribes or purchase fraudulent documents. INS made little effort to locate or deport aliens who were the customers and beneficiaries of document fraud schemes. INS did not take action to preclude such aliens from receiving benefits for which their fraud had made them eligible; did not act to delete, correct, or flag fraudulent entries in its automated data bases and information systems; and had no provision for placing any code, flag or alert in INS records to warn INS officers should they encounter these same aliens in the future."

According to the Congressional Research Service of the Library of Congress prior the 1996 Welfare Reform Act, immigrants were participating in more than fifteen major federal and State programs. These included Aid to Families with Dependent Children (AFDC); Supplemental Security Income (SSI); General Assistance; Housing and Urban Development; Community Development Grants, Foster care, adoption assistance, and child welfare; Medicaid, emergency services and services for pregnant women; State and local medical care; School lunch and breakfast programs; Headstart, Job Training Partnership Act; Title IV for Higher Education; Block grants for social services; Adult Education Grants; Women, Infants, and Children (WIC), and Home Energy Assistance.

> ***"As the source of U.S. immigration was switched by the 1965 immigration act away from Europe and to the Third World, immigrant welfare dependency rates have risen noticeably."***

In addition, immigrants also participate in the Earned-Income Tax Credit (EITC). Under this program, if one's income is below a prescribed level the federal government will issue that individual a refund check even if no income tax is due. In 1996, a recipient could receive a maximum of $3,556. Although eligibility is restricted to U.S. citizens and legal resident aliens, the Internal Revenue Service, nevertheless, does not hamper illegal aliens from receiving these refunds. If an applicant supplies a Social Security number that cannot be processed because it is false—and a preliminary 1992 report by the Immigration and Naturalization Service found 83 percent of illegal aliens amnestied by the Immigration and Reform Act (IRCA) had false Social Security numbers—it is not uncommon for the Internal Revenue Service to issue that person a temporary number so a refund check can still be dispatched.

The Immigrant Burden on Welfare

As the source of U. S. immigration was switched by the 1965 immigration act away from Europe and to the Third World, immigrant welfare dependency rates have risen noticeably. In 1970, immigrant participation in welfare was comparable to native-born Americans—6 percent. By 1990, however, immigrant welfare participation rates were, on average, higher than native-born Americans in general (9 percent versus 7 percent) and higher still than "white, non-Hispanic" native-born Americans, i.e., European-Americans, in particular, whose welfare participation rate was estimated at around 5 percent.

"Because more recent immigrant waves start off poorly, it is unlikely that the earnings of the 'new immigrants' will ever catch up with those of natives."

For specific immigrant groups, the welfare dependency rate is higher, sometimes dramatically higher: Chinese and Filipinos—10 percent, Mexicans—11 percent, Ecuadorians—12 percent, pre-Marielito Cubans—15 percent, Vietnamese—26 percent, Dominicans—28 percent, and Cambodians and Laotians—nearly 50 percent.

During this same period, immigrants went from being the recipients of 7 percent of all welfare cash benefits in 1970 to 13 percent in 1990. But three-quarters of the total cost of welfare is "non-cash transfers." These "non-cash transfers" include such programs as the previously listed Aid to Families with Dependent Children (AFDC), Supplemental Security Income (SSI), Housing Assistance, Medicaid, Student Lunch Programs, Women, Infants, and Children (WIC), as well as Food Stamps.

When those programs were examined, Dr. George Borjas of Harvard University found that although immigrants are 9 percent of the U.S population they accounted for 12 percent of the costs of Food Stamps, 14 percent of the costs of Medicaid, 17 percent of the costs of Aid to Families with Dependent Children (AFDC), 18 percent of the costs of Supplemental Security Income (SSI), and 19 percent of the costs of school breakfasts and lunches.

Factoring in "non-cash transfers," Dr. Borjas discovered that the overall welfare dependency rate for immigrants is really 21 percent compared to 14 percent for native-born Americans and 11 percent for "white, non-Hispanic" native-born Americans—i.e., European-Americans. Immigrants' use of welfare, therefore, is 50 percent higher than native-born Americans and approximately 90 percent higher than "white, non-Hispanic" native-born Americans—i.e., European-Americans.

Fewer Skills and Less Education

This growth in welfare dependency by immigrants is expected to continue since current immigrants have less schooling, less proficiency in the English language, less skills, and are earning less than either earlier immigrants or native-born Americans.

Nearly 40 percent of all adults admitted to the United States each year are high school dropouts. By 1990, one of every four immigrants from Mexico who were of high school age were not attending school, and an estimated total of 3.06 million immigrant high school dropouts were residing in the United States accounting for one-fifth of all high school dropouts in the national labor market. This represented a doubling of the immigrant share of high school dropouts since just 1980. Furthermore, between 1990 and 1995, an additional 1.05 million adult high school dropouts were legally admitted to the United States.

Among illegal aliens 24 years old or older amnestied between 1989 and 1992 by the Immigration and Reform Control Act (IRCA), 28 percent were high school dropouts while another 55 percent had never attended high school.

In addition, current immigrants are less proficient in the English language. The 1990 Census found that among the foreign born those who entered the United States since 1980 approximately 42 percent were "linguistically isolated"—i.e., living in "households in which no one 14 years old or over speaks only English and no one who speaks a language other than English speaks English 'very well'"—compared to only 18 percent among those who entered before 1980.

Of the foreign born who arrived since 1980, 60 percent do not speak English "very well" compared to 37 percent of those who arrived before 1980. Among the foreign born, only 26 percent of Europeans do not speak English "very well" compared to 71 percent of Mexicans, 63 percent of Central Americans, 48 percent of South Americans, and 43 percent of Caribbean islanders.

By 1992, only 36 percent of all the illegal aliens amnestied by the Immigration and Reform Control Act (IRCA) since 1989 claimed they spoke English well. The majority of those amnestied were Mexican and only 27 percent of them reported that they could speak English well.

Permanent Welfare Recipients

According to Dr. Borjas, "Because more recent immigrant waves start off poorly, it is unlikely that the earnings of the 'new immigrants' will ever catch up with those of natives. In fact, the wage differential between immigrants and natives may exceed 20 percent even after two or three decades after immigration."

In his 1990 book, *Friends or Strangers*, Dr. Borjas wrote that "The skill level of successive immigrants waves admitted to the U.S. has declined precipitously in the past two or three decades." Six years later in his article, "Immigration and the Welfare State: Immigrant Participation in Means-Tested Entitlement Programs," Dr. Borjas noted that "immigrants are more likely to be exposed to the welfare system and are more likely to become 'permanent' recipients."

By 1990, immigrants were earning, on average, 16 percent less than native-born Americans. But those immigrants who arrived after 1985 were actually earning 32 percent less than native-born Americans. By 1995, the poverty rate for the foreign-born was 70 percent higher than that for native-born Americans.

Dr. Borjas has calculated that the influx of such immigrants has been responsible for a third of the decline in the wages of native-born unskilled workers nationwide during the 1980s, an annual displacement of 2.3 million mostly unskilled and low skilled workers, and an annual cost of $133 billion in depressed wages.

The Impact on California

The impact of current immigration has been felt most acutely in California. Within twenty years, the distribution of skills in the State deteriorated to a phenomenal degree. In 1970, California possessed workers that were 50 percent more likely to be skilled than those in the United States as a whole. By 1990, however, California workers were now 50 percent more likely to be less skilled than those in the rest of the country. And immigrants accounted for 85 percent of all male workers with fewer than nine years of education.

In California, immigrant households now receive 40 percent of all cash and noncash welfare benefits. This has led Dr. Borjas to assert that "It is not too much of an exaggeration to say that the welfare problem in California is on the verge of becoming an immigrant problem."

"The net national cost of immigration to the U.S. taxpayers was $65 billion a year in 1996, or the equivalent of costing every U.S. family of four $981."

In addition, "the recent elderly immigrant population (those residing in the U.S. for less than 20 years) more than tripled between 1970 and 1994." A study by Dr. Donald L. Huddle of Rice University and David Simcox, Senior Fellow at the Center for Immigration Studies, found that immigrants were receiving more in social security benefits than they contributed to the program, thereby resulting in a $2.7 billion deficit in 1992. They estimate that over the next decade the social security deficit caused by immigration will total $30 billion.

Furthermore, in just the twelve years from 1982 to 1994, the number of elderly immigrants who received Supplementary Security Income (SSI) increased from 127,900 to 738,000 or by approximately 580 percent. If this trend continues, it is projected that by the year 2004 this number will increase to more than 3 million, the SSI and Medicaid benefits received by these immigrants will amount to $328 billion, and the cost of providing these benefits will exceed $67 billion a year. In 1994, immigrants received nearly half, 49 percent, of all Supplementary Security Income (SSI) payments and their average monthly benefits were double the amount paid to U.S. citizens. Remarkably, 25 percent of those immigrants receiving Supplementary Security Income (SSI) payments belong to families who had yearly incomes in excess of $64,000.

According to the findings of Dr. Huddle, the net national cost of immigration to the U.S. taxpayers was $65 billion a year in 1996, or the equivalent of costing every U.S. family of four $981. This is significantly higher than the $46 billion it cost in 1992 and is an increase of 40 percent in just four years. This cost is projected to grow to $108 billion annually within the decade.

A contributing factor to this rising cost of immigration has been the impact of the amnesty awarded to approximately 3 million illegal aliens by the Immigration and Control Act (IRCA) of 1986. Between 1987 and 1996, the total net fiscal deficit caused by these amnesties was nearly $79 billion. This was the equivalent of giving each one of the nearly 3 million illegal aliens amnestied a check for over $25,000. The direct costs incurred by this amnesty program were $24 billion, while indirect costs—i.e., job displacement, public education, and public assistance programs to citizen children 18 and under—amounted to another $55 billion and are still growing.

Illegal Immigration Harms Low-Wage Workers

by Richard Estrada

About the author: *Richard Estrada is a columnist for the* Dallas Morning News.

America's immigration system has for decades stuck in the craw of many citizens who cherish democracy and the rule of law. By increasingly caving in to special interests who are indifferent to, or supportive of, illegal immigration, the federal government has turned the nonenforcement of immigration laws into an art form.

Lax Border Enforcement

But the Clinton administration is embroidering even that situation in 1999. When the government agency charged with excluding unauthorized workers from the labor market begins downplaying work-site inspections and refusing reinforcements to reduce illegal entries, the word "concern" fails.

As chief overseer of the Immigration and Naturalization Service [INS], Attorney General Janet Reno told Congress that she has decided against requesting an additional 1,000 Border Patrol agents that Congress had already authorized. It is as if she was minimizing the danger of unauthorized border crossings.

Illegal immigration once plagued the California–Mexico border more than anywhere else until more guards were added there. But today, the border crashing has shifted to southern Arizona. Patrolling the northern border with Canada is no longer a walk in the park, either—what with the arrest of terrorist suspects and an increase in drug and alien smuggling.

But Reno waves such worries away with the argument of good bureaucratic management. She says that bringing on too many rookies too quickly threatens the professionalism and integrity of the Border Patrol.

The argument seems bizarre. It is as if President Roosevelt had argued at the outset of World War II that the U.S. armed forces could only absorb so many green recruits at one time, so he had decided to suspend the draft temporarily. You cannot ignore undocumented workers without also ignoring drug thugs and terrorists.

Playing Politics

The administration did beef up the Border Patrol in 1996, after being pressured by Congress. Given the administration's record of playing politics with naturalizing immigrants too hastily in 1996, a move that some interpreted as a brazen attempt to curry favor with immigration lawyers and ethnic politicians, Reno's latest decision could be explained by the lack of a presidential election this year.

Political pressure may be another factor. Several months ago, onion growers in Vidalia, Ga., called upon various Georgia congressmen and the state's two senators to persuade the INS to go fishing during the onion harvest. The plantation politicos in Congress succeeded in diluting immigration law enforcement.

Agribusiness employers routinely claim not to knowingly hire undocumented workers. But they then argue that their livelihood depends on the INS suspending the enforcement of laws against knowingly hiring undocumented workers.

Illegal Immigration Hurts the Poor and Dispossessed

The travesty undermines no one in America more than black and Hispanic citizens and legal residents. Legal migrant workers have for decades suffered competition from undocumented workers in the fields, from Florida to California. That never-ending stream of inexpensive undocumented labor helps explain why low wages and abysmal working conditions remain stagnant.

A recent article in *The Wall Street Journal* unwittingly underscored the challenge in urban America. The piece noted that the "spectacular" economy of the past eight years has largely bypassed one group in particular: Almost 32 percent of black male teenagers who want jobs can't get them, compared with 12.2 percent of their white counterparts.

Sure, racism plays a role. But given that undocumented immigrants overwhelmingly settle in the largest cities of six or seven states, they are bound to pose severe competition for the young blacks in those locales. Labor market experts not quoted by the laissez-faire *Journal* made this point a few days ago in testimony before the House immigration subcommittee. Still, as the Labor Department terms young black males looking for work "the most disadvantaged group in the country," the INS increasingly chooses to take a powder.

Many members of Congress could care less. Even before Reno began downgrading enforcement, they had already blocked a system whereby employers would call a central data bank, enter the Social Security number provided by the job applicant, and await a yes or no answer, with a confirmation code.

The situation is made worse when the government itself begins winking at the immigration laws. That is evidence that the political fix is in. Profits are guaranteed, while America's own poor and dispossessed are denied an honest chance at working their way up the socioeconomic ladder. Especially in this turbocharged economy, the current scenario is the shame of the nation.

Illegal Immigration Poses a Terrorist Threat to the United States

by Samuel Francis

About the author: *Samuel Francis is a syndicated columnist.*

Editor's Note: In the following viewpoint, Samuel Francis suggests that the crash of TWA flight 800 could have been the result of a terrorist attack. At press time, investigators had not confirmed that the aircraft was bombed.

Was the 1996 destruction of TWA Flight 800 and the death of its 229 passengers an act of sabotage and mass murder? No one yet knows, but so far most experts seem to think sabotage is not unlikely. What hardly anyone is willing to think—or at least say—is that the country's uncontrolled immigration crisis makes such acts of terror far easier than most Americans realize.

Operation Dustmop

One reason nations ought to take border security seriously is that, if they don't, all sorts of undesirable elements can cross their borders. In 1996 the Immigration and Naturalization Service (INS) happened to round up quite a few such elements—at an international airport.

The airport was Newark International, not too far from Kennedy International, from which Flight 800 took wing four months later. At Newark, the INS nabbed no fewer than 112 illegal aliens working as contract cleaners for a Newark cleaning firm.

As the INS news release of March 31st put it, "The investigation, known as 'Operation Dustmop,' targeted undocumented aliens using false documents to obtain security passes which would allow them to clean both terminals and aircraft at Newark Airport." It doesn't require a lot of imagination to understand that low-level cleaning employees who spruce up the interiors of airplanes

Reprinted from "Uncontrolled Immigration Creates Terrorist Threat," by Samuel Francis, *The Wanderer,* August 8, 1996. Reprinted with permission from Samuel Francis and Creators Syndicate.

might add to the decor by stashing a few explosives in the right spot. The ease with which false documents, not only for identification but also for security passes, can be obtained merely increases the danger.

"The aliens encountered," the news release continued, "were from a variety of countries including Ecuador, Peru, Guatemala, Brazil, Honduras, Colombia, Portugal, and Spain." Most of those countries now or in the recent past have had active terrorist organizations, and not a few of them enjoy the presence of transnational drug cartels, which have been known to blow up airlines' jets.

Ten Wanted Criminal Aliens

It is now well known that criminal types are not exactly rare among immigrants these days. Some 25% of the federal prison system is inhabited by aliens, and in July, 1996 the INS released a list of "Ten Wanted Criminal Aliens" as a kind of immigration equivalent to the FBI's long-standing "Ten Most Wanted" list of domestic criminals.

And, while both political parties in Congress ignore the immigration crisis, alien crime is swelling. From California comes news of dramatic increases in the number of alien criminal arrests. In the state's Northern District, federal felony cases filed increased by nearly 48% last year, and 24% of the increase involved immigrants. In the Southern District, immigration-related felonies made up nearly 58% of all federal criminal cases.

> ***"The country's uncontrolled immigration crisis makes . . . acts of terror far easier than most Americans realize."***

Foreign organized crime syndicates are common enough in the immigration wave—not only Colombian and Jamaican drug gangs, but also the Japanese Yakuza, Chinese Triad Societies, and Russian, Nigerian, and even Israeli mafias. Some years ago, the Drug Enforcement Administration reported that "ethnic gangs appear to be 'the' new trend in crime," and "ethnic" in this context usually means "immigrant."

Alien Terrorists

Then there are the terrorists themselves as opposed to good, old-fashioned hoodlums. Back in the 1980s, national security officials repeatedly warned against the infiltration of our borders by alien terrorists, and some members of terrorist groups actually turned up trying to cross the border. The bombing of the World Trade Center in 1993 by Islamic terrorists is one terrorist atrocity committed by aliens. So probably was the murder of two CIA employees in 1996 by a Pakistani. And the still-unknown "John Doe II" of the Oklahoma City bombing in 1995 may have been an alien who left the country after the act of mass murder.

Even if aliens (and their American pals) aren't blowing up major targets like airliners and Manhattan skyscrapers, they're often in the front lines of political violence, as in the recent attack on peaceful demonstrators against illegal immigration in Los Angeles by the Communist Progressive Labor Party and its left-wing allies in the immigration lobby.

During the controversy over California's Proposition 187, supporters of the anti-immigration measure were often attacked by violent mobs and counter-demonstrators, and southern California in particular sports a small army of Latin American separatists who seek the breakup of the United States and the return of the American southwest to Mexico.

Despite the absence of hard evidence that Flight 800 was the victim of a terrorist attack, boosters of big government are already beating the drums for an antiterrorist "supercommand" that can zip around the globe to mete out vengeance against their enemies, and forking over more power to the FBI and other federal police for "counterterrorism" remains one of their favorite remedies. But before we give up any more of the freedoms of Americans, maybe we ought to consider the simpler solution of just controlling our borders and keeping out people who have none but criminal reasons for wanting to come here.

Illegal Immigration Harms the Border Environment

by Carey Goldberg

About the author: *Carey Goldberg is a staff writer for the* New York Times.

In some canyons [at Otay Mountain in California], it looks as if hundreds of Hansels and Gretels have scattered trails of trash behind them, marking the route from Tijuana.

Halloweenish Landscapes

New paths fork across almost every slope, giving parts of this once-lonely mountain the threadbare look of the more trafficked corners of a city park.

And a 15,000-acre swath of the mountain ridge is stripped and sooty, burned in October 1996 to a Halloweenish landscape of naked black branches and orange dust by a wildfire that the authorities are convinced was sparked by an illegal border-crosser. Who else, they ask, would have been desperate enough to be up on a 4,000-foot peak building a campfire here on a windy autumn night?

"I've never seen an area like this before," said Jo Simpson, assistant district manager for the Federal Bureau of Land Management. "It's just been trashed. They've cut numerous trails, so that degraded it, and the ultimate degradation was when they burnt it."

As the Federal Government has tried, in 1995 and 1996, to stem the stream of illegal immigration near San Diego, the battle has spread to this forbidding stretch of public land, a range of heights and draws 15 miles east of the Pacific Ocean.

Perilous Treks

Clandestine crossers who once hopped a fence near the ocean at the edge of Tijuana's urban sprawl now face beefed-up patrols and barriers. So they have been turning to perilous treks of five or six miles through these mountains, risking heat exhaustion in summer highs of 110 degrees, bandits, snakes and thirst.

Initial Government plans for the region had figured the terrain would be enough to stop most illegal crossers here. They were wrong.

Instead, the traffic in the Otay Mountain area has set off a striking side-skirmish in the border war. The immigrants are taking to these mountains in such numbers—hundreds each night, it is estimated—that nature lovers and Government officials warn that they are threatening the environment here.

A Biological Jewel

"It's a biological jewel," Nick Ervin, desert committee chairman of the San Diego Sierra Club, said of the Otay Mountain region. "The Tecate cypress exists almost nowhere else in the world and it's in abundance on Otay Mountain, which is a prime area for several rare and endangered plants. And now the area's being largely ruined."

Much of the Otay Mountain environs are officially designated by the Department of the Interior as a protected Wilderness Study Area because of those rare plants. Unfortunately, the plants tend to grow in the very canyon beds where the illegal immigrants tread, their feet grinding down the root systems of the fragile growths. The fires, a vast majority of which are caused by campfires, also have environmentalists and Government officials worried; though fires are part of the natural cycle here, they are becoming so frequent that they threaten to wipe some plants out, Mr. Ervin said.

> ***"Nature lovers and Government officials warn that [illegal immigrants] are threatening the environment."***

More than 322 fires have been spotted in the Otay Mountain area in 1996, said Richard D. Franklin, the Interior Department's chief of fire and aviation management for the California desert region. His firefighters have taken to helicopter flights three times a week to find the remains of the campfires the illegal immigrants leave, he said. Out of fear that immigrants will be trapped and killed in the blazes, they spend hundreds of thousands of dollars extinguishing fires they would normally have let burn out naturally.

San Diego County officials, afraid that they might have to foot the bill for treating burn victims in these mountains, declared a state of emergency here this summer to attract more state and Federal money, and Federal officials have erected several signs on the most traveled Otay footpaths, warning in Spanish: "It is difficult to escape a fire in action."

Economic Push and Pull

It is even more difficult to stop the flow of people leaving the economic deprivation of Mexico for the under-the-table jobs waiting for them in the United States. The Border Patrol has almost doubled the personnel in its San Diego sector since 1993, to nearly 2,000 agents, and is catching a half-million illegal immigrants a year.

But "the economic push and pull are so incredible that it's like you hear a giant sucking sound," said Jim Pilkington, a Border Patrol agent and spokesman.

The power of that pull became clear when Pedro Acosta, 43, and Francisco Arroyo, 30, two Mexicans caught by the Border Patrol just after they had made it over the mountain, described the terrors of their trip. They spoke from a Border Patrol van on their way to be processed and deported.

"Out of fear that immigrants will be trapped and killed in the blazes, [firefighters] spend hundreds of thousands of dollars extinguishing fires they would normally have let burn out naturally."

"We're very afraid of the journey," said Mr. Acosta, a gardener who had been on his way to an American job from his hometown of Sinaloa. "There are people who don't make it—and if you get lost in the mountains and can't find your way, you remain there."

Mr. Arroyo, 30, said, "You can fall, there are the bandits, the snakes and lots of people die when there is fire."

Both men looked exhausted after an all-night trek up miles of rugged slopes. Although some immigrants hire guides to help them with the crossing, Mr. Acosta and Mr. Arroyo said they had not.

In the last two years, the Border Patrol has recorded more than 20 immigrants' deaths in the region, most from exposure. They have also noticed that almost all the crossers they catch now are young men, since most women and children no longer try the mountain ordeal.

The patrol is trying to stop even that traffic, pouring dozens of new agents into the area.

No one expects a quick end to the illegal foot traffic, but environmentalists hope that one of these days, the area might again be safe enough to hike in without fear of meeting up with bandits, border police officers or quick-moving wildfires.

But for now, Mr. Ervin said, hikers say, "There's no way I'm going to Otay Mountain—it's a war zone."

Illegal Aliens Gain Clout: Tight Labor Market Changes Thinking of Unions and Employers

by Timothy Burn

About the author: *Timothy Burn writes for the* Washington Times.

Life has changed for Armando Torres, an illegal immigrant who walked across the southern border into the United States four years ago.

Mr. Torres in those years has been transformed from an out-of-work husband and father struggling to survive in his home of Chihuahua, Mexico, to a man who is wanted all across America.

He's wanted by employers and labor unions and increasingly is acknowledged as an essential component of the booming U.S. economy.

Perhaps for the first time in his life, the 29-year-old construction worker and Atlanta resident has clout.

Construction companies want him to help feed America's raging demand for new homes. And now unions want him to join their ranks to help fight for better wages and pay for all workers.

A few years ago Mr. Torres was impoverished. Now he earns about $800 a week pouring concrete and doing other construction work that an increasing number of Americans simply do not want to do anymore.

"I came out of necessity to the land of opportunity," says Mr. Torres, who was lured into the United States by an Atlanta construction company owner who promised good pay for a good day's work, no questions asked.

Speaking through an interpreter, Mr. Torres adds: "One day I just crossed the border with a friend. And then it took me a year to get my family across."

The stark changes in those four years reflect an equally dramatic shift during that time in the way America views illegal immigrants. The shift means many

Reprinted from "Illegal Aliens Gain Clout: Tight Labor Market Changes Thinking of Unions and Employers," by Timothy Burn, *The Washington Times,* June 4, 2000. Reprinted with permission from *The Washington Times.* Visit their web site at www.washtimes.com.

are pushing for changes in immigration law to make it easier for others like Mr. Torres to live and work in the United States.

The tight labor market—with the unemployment rate now at 4.1 percent—is forcing the United States to take a second look at how it addresses immigration. More than ever, immigrants both legal and illegal are in demand for jobs from construction laborer to computer programmer.

Many in business, labor, the Clinton administration, and Congress believe a complete overhaul of immigration laws is just around the corner.

Rough Road

Despite his new clout in the U.S. workplace, Mr. Torres' journey—like others—has been tough. As he tells it, that journey involved long, thankless hours and unscrupulous employers who exploited him under thinly veiled threats of deportation.

Mr. Torres was one of about 20 Mexican men, all illegal, who went to work for V.C. Lovell, owner of Universal Concrete Wall of Cornelia, Ga.

Mr. Torres says he was paid $250 each week, which seemed adequate compared with Mexican wages. But soon he realized that 60 hours of hard construction work was worth much more than that.

As with most occupations, the average weekly wage for construction workers has climbed in recent years. The average weekly wage for those workers was $688.16 in April, up 5.8 percent from a year earlier, according to the Bureau of Labor Statistics. The average weekly wage for all private-sector jobs rose to $474.37 in April, up 5.1 percent from April 1999.

Mr. Torres and his colleagues were reluctant to speak out since their employer seemed to hold all the cards. He says that not only were they forced to work long hours, but also they were given few breaks and little water as they toiled in the hot Georgia sun.

"Pretty much when you go to work, there are no rights," Mr. Torres says. "There is nothing you can do. You are just a body."

"The tight labor market . . . is forcing the United States to take a second look at how it addresses immigration . . . Immigrants both legal and illegal are in demand for jobs."

Now, like a growing number of his co-workers, he is standing up and demanding better treatment for undocumented employees. The men recently voted unanimously to join the United Brotherhood of Carpenters and Joiners of America.

"The day of the election, the boss said if you come to vote there could be an INS bus waiting for you," Mr. Torres recalls. "We just got valor and went and voted anyway. After the elections we felt strong because we won."

Mr. Lovell says Mr. Torres was paid $10 per hour, allowed restroom breaks at any time and given all the water he wanted. And Mr. Lovell denies ever threatening to report Mexican workers to the INS, although he declines to comment further.

Disputes between employers and undocumented workers are increasingly common, labor groups say. The Washington area's immigrant workforce has swelled in recent years amid strong economic growth. Many of those who come to the area find work, but often with lower pay and few guarantees of fair treatment.

Each weekday before dawn scores of Hispanic men, most of them illegal aliens, gather in front of the 7-Eleven store in Bailey's Crossroads waiting for work.

> ***"Pretty much when [undocumented workers] go to work, there are no rights. . . . There is nothing you can do. You are just a body."***

One of the men waiting there on a recent day is Oscar, 32, an illegal immigrant from El Salvador who arrived in the United States in search of opportunity and asks that his last name not be published.

"Virginia is booming, but the type of treatment we receive has become worse," Oscar says. "Actually, Virginia is being built by us."

He says he and fellow workers plan to unionize for better pay and working conditions.

"I saw eight to 10 bad accidents, guys falling off the roof and such, " he says. "The contractors, they are afraid of getting sued. They give them a couple hundred dollars, drop them off and never come back."

Changing Times

Businesses large and small, from construction to high-tech, are producing on all cylinders and struggling to find and keep workers to maintain the boom.

Though most employers obey the law by turning away undocumented workers, many continue to hire illegal aliens, casting a blind eye on counterfeit documentation. Some also exploit illegal aliens, taking advantage of their often minimal command of English or lack of knowledge of their rights.

Even as staff-strapped employers increasingly look to illegal aliens for help, the Clinton administration is taking a fresh look at the role of undocumented workers.

No longer just interested in finding ways to keep illegal aliens out, the federal government is stepping up efforts to protect them from discrimination once they enter the work force. And the administration says it wants to make it easier for more illegal residents to gain permanent status.

"I think that over the next five years Congress will be compelled to significantly rewrite immigration policy," says Frank Sharry, executive director of the Washington-based National Immigration Forum, a group that advocates open immigration.

"The new dynamics in place are that our population is aging, and job growth is outstripping labor force growth," Mr. Sharry says. "To me it is not a question of if, but of how, we will reform immigration."

Others note that the mood of the nation has changed toward illegal immigrants in the past few years as the economy has remained strong.

"The tight labor market certainly has softened the rhetoric of those who oppose more open immigration," says Jeffrey S. Passel, an immigration specialist at the Urban Institute, which is neutral on the issue.

Still, immigration remains a touchy subject among politicians and is low on the list of talking points of the two leading presidential candidates. An aide to Texas Gov. George W. Bush said the Republican presidential hopeful supports moves in Congress to boost guest worker visas for high-tech companies. Mr. Bush generally favors more open immigration policies.

Vice President Al Gore, meanwhile, supports administration efforts to protect the rights of illegal immigrants. But the Democrat's presidential campaign has not issued its position on guest worker visas.

Had Mr. Torres crossed America's southern border a few years earlier, he would have entered a nation still reeling from the recession of the early '90s and in no mood to accommodate new arrivals like him.

Now, just a few years after Congress in 1996 tightened restrictions on immigration and California passed a ballot initiative slashing services for illegal immigrants,[1] business and labor groups are urging policy-makers to make it easier to work in the United States.

"For both businesses and labor, opening America's borders is a matter of survival."

"It is hard now to make the claim that illegal immigrants are expensive in terms of their impact on public-sector spending," Mr. Passel says, noting that five years ago the influx of undocumented workers was blamed for California's budget deficit.

"Now California, like virtually every other state, is running a surplus. Those arguments can no longer be made, at least not with a straight face," he says.

That's welcome news for illegal immigrants. But they also want fair treatment on the job.

Ripe for Change

Both Congress and President Bill Clinton are listening.

Signaling the new administration effort on behalf of illegal residents, the Equal Employment Opportunity Commission in October issued a "clarification" intended to remind both employers and employees that all workers, including the undocumented, are protected against discrimination under Title VII of the Civil Rights Act of 1964.

And in April [2000], the Immigration and Naturalization Service announced it would allow seven undocumented Mexican hotel workers to stay in the United States for another two years. The INS granted them the unusual extension because of their role in a landmark discrimination case against their employer, the Holiday Inn Express in Minneapolis.

The hotel workers claimed their employer exploited them under thinly veiled threats of deportation. They joined a union, and their boss in turn reported them to the INS.

The Clinton administration, meanwhile, wants to distribute an extra 362,500 visas over the next three years to more immigrants fleeing political strife. Nicaraguans and Cubans are given preference over nationals from countries like El Salvador, Guatemala, Honduras and Haiti, even though immigrants from those countries often seek to adjust their status claiming political persecution.

The president also wants to create a new deadline for long-term illegal residents to seek legal status. Currently only immigrants who arrived prior to 1972 can apply for permanent residency. Mr. Clinton would move that date up to 1986, allowing many more illegal immigrants the opportunity to become legal.

The administration has linked the president's plan to proposals in Congress to boost guest worker visas.

Americans, and many legalized immigrants, tend to oppose loosening immigration laws, fearing their jobs will be taken away and their standard of living will decline. And in the 2000 election year, Congress is wary of upsetting the public with broad liberalization of immigration laws.

But for both businesses and labor, opening America's borders is a matter of survival. Lobbyists from both camps are pushing aggressively for change on several fronts.

"For unions, the interest is in ensuring that immigrant workers here feel free to assert their labor rights," says the National Immigration Forum's Mr. Sharry. "For business lobbies, they want to increase immigration to have more workers."

Changes in immigration law already are taking place incrementally. Mr. Sharry and others believe the time is ripe for a complete overhaul of immigration laws.

"We do need a fresh look because we need an immigration policy that better serves America's interests," says Rep. Lamar Smith, Texas Republican and chairman of the House Judiciary immigration subcommittee. "We simply do not admit enough people with the skills we need in our work force."

Mr. Smith says, however, that too many unskilled workers are entering the United States, jeopardizing neighborhoods and putting a burden on government services.

Mr. Smith and several other lawmakers instead are focusing on trying to admit more foreign workers with higher educations and technology training, which they believe will help the economy and ease the worker shortage in the booming high-tech industry.

High-tech companies are pushing Congress to allow more skilled foreign professionals to enter the United States temporarily through the H-1B visa program. Under intense pressure from companies in Silicon Valley to the Dulles Corridor in 1998, Congress raised the cap on the number of such visas granted to employers temporarily to 115,000 a year.

That cap was reached in the first quarter this year, and now those companies want the amount boosted further. Claiming that its industry is suffering from a potentially debilitating worker shortage, the Information Technology Association of America estimates that high-tech companies will have about 850,000 jobs unfilled in the next year.

> ***"The hospitality industry is drafting plans to lobby Congress to raise the limit on unskilled workers entering the United States."***

One proposal under consideration in Congress would raise the cap to 200,000 each year until 2002. Both Congress and the administration, eager to please the engine of the new economy and newfound campaign contributors, appear ready to listen.

High-tech companies are not the only ones complaining to Congress about a shortage of workers.

Restaurants and hotels are hanging "help wanted" signs all over the nation, and they say fewer applicants are walking in. Following the lead of high-tech groups, the hospitality industry is drafting plans to lobby Congress to raise the limit on unskilled workers entering the United States under the H-2B visa program.

"It is really hard to find workers in the restaurant business because most Americans just aren't applying," says Pam Felix, owner of California Tortilla in Bethesda. "I never get Americans applying for busboy or cook spots. Immigrants are filling the majority of those positions."

Ms. Felix says about two-thirds of her staff are immigrants, mainly from Africa and Central America.

"They are such wonderful workers. They work so hard at their jobs and at learning English. We have been very lucky."

She says some Americans she has talked to believe most immigrants go on welfare after entering the country.

"Certainly in my experience that couldn't be further from the truth. People think Americans are applying for these jobs, and they are not."

She pays between $7 and $12 per hour, with full health and dental benefits.

Ms. Felix supports efforts to make it easier for illegal immigrants to stay and work in the United States. "It would be wonderful. We have to turn so many people away because they have fake IDs," she says.

The Future of Labor

The nation's labor unions, meanwhile, also have changed the way they think about immigrants.

Unions gradually have lost power in the American workplace as membership has declined in the past two decades. While aggressive organizing in the past two years has stopped the hemorrhaging, unions still struggle to find new pools of potential members.

Part of the decline stems from the shift from manufacturing to a service-based economy. But union efforts to organize lower-rung workers—from farm workers to hotel workers—also have been hampered by the steady influx of illegal immigrants crossing into the United States to work in those fields for subpar wages.

Labor traditionally has viewed illegal immigrants as a threat to membership. But now union organizers believe undocumented workers may hold the key to their survival.

In a major shift, the AFL-CIO union in February called for a restructuring of immigration law to improve the rights of undocumented workers by granting them the right to stay in the country and work permanently. And it is calling for an end to sanctions against employers who hire illegal aliens.

Illegal immigrants are pouring into the United States in ever greater numbers. While no one knows exactly how large America's immigrant work force is, the INS says nearly 700,000 immigrants were allowed into the country for permanent residence in 1998.

A month ago, Mr. Torres and other illegal immigrants from Central America to Somalia participated in a forum in Atlanta sponsored by the AFL-CIO and intended to build support among rank-and-file members for labor's new push to legalize and organize undocumented workers.

Michael Monroe, president of the Painters and Allied Trades Unions, says that for far too long the nation's unions turned their backs on nonwhite, nonmale workers.

Listening to Mr. Torres' stories of how he was forced to work 60-hour weeks for $250, denied bathroom breaks and threatened with deportation, Mr. Monroe says it was time for unions to stand with immigrant workers.

"My union is over 100 years old. My union is overwhelmingly white. My union is overwhelmingly male. In my opinion as a lifelong union member, organized labor is as much at fault for the stories you are hearing today as management is," he says.

"We apologize for any lateness in coming on this scene," he adds. "But we are here now, and we are going to be here with you because we want all of you in our unions."

With both business and unions calling for a more liberal immigration policy, many believe that Congress will be compelled to act. Proponents of more open immigration believe that recent statements on the matter by Federal Reserve Chairman Alan Greenspan will give lawmakers the push they need.

Mr. Greenspan, testifying in January 2000 before the Senate Banking Committee, said: " . . . I think reviewing our immigration laws in the context of the type of economy which we will be enjoying in the decade ahead is clearly on the table in my judgment."

Illegal Immigration from Mexico Provides a Long-Term Benefit to the United States

by Aurelio Rojas

About the author: *Aurelio Rojas is a staff writer for the* San Francisco Chronicle.

The nation's first long-term study to examine how long immigrants from Mexico remain in the United States has concluded that, contrary to public perception, most return home.

Most Undocumented Immigrants Return Home

Findings released in 1997 by the Public Policy Institute of California show that about half of the immigrants studied during a 10-year period returned to Mexico within two years. Far more, almost 70 percent, returned within 10 years.

In addition to interviews with more than 43,000 people from six Mexican states, researchers analyzed data previously collected by a group called the Mexican Migration Project. That data showed that return rates are even higher for undocumented immigrants—only about 27 percent of the roughly 214,000 undocumented immigrants who entered California from western Mexico between 1980 and 1990 remain or will remain in the United States after 10 years, the researchers concluded.

Men are more likely than women to return home, as are people with little education and agricultural workers, the study said.

A Long-Term Gain

The study, which comes at a time of great public debate over whether immigrants help or hurt the economy, suggests that immigrants represent a long-term gain to society because those who are better off tend to stay, while most who are poor return to Mexico.

"Immigrants may impose a net cost on government services the first year they are here, but over 10 years or more, they provide long-term benefits because more low wage-earners return home, and those with a higher taxable income settle down in the United States," said economist Belinda Reyes, who headed the study.

Reyes said that policymakers in California and the rest of the nation need to consider that immigrants leave the country as well as arrive; to ignore this fact, she said, is to "run the risk of making decisions based on inaccurate data or faulty assumptions."

But Ira Mehlman, the West Coast representative of the Federation for Immigration Reform, said that policymakers already understand that some immigrants leave.

"It's always been true that many immigrants return home, but a significant number stay. And it's the cumulative effect that worries us," Mehlman said. "How long can the United States continue to absorb 300,000 to 500,000 illegal immigrants a year?"

"Illegal immigrants 'provide long-term benefits because more low wage-earners return home, and those with a higher taxable income settle down in the United States.'"

According to the study, some 60 percent of all Mexican immigrants to the United States have come from the six Mexican states of Durango, Guanajuato, Jalisco, Michoacan, Zacatecas and Nayarit.

No Drain on Social Services

Of those studied, researchers found:

• 54 percent entered the United States illegally.

• Those who immigrated to California stayed in the United States longer than those who immigrated to other states.

• Most immigrants do not stay long enough to be eligible for social services. (The laws regulating such time limits are currently in flux.)

"The majority of immigrants from western Mexico come here without family and stay only a short time," Reyes said. "The one-third who remain over the long term are the most likely to succeed in the U.S. labor market."

Chapter 3

Does the United States Treat Illegal Immigrants Fairly?

Chapter Preface

Sixty-six-year-old Andrés Román Díaz walked home from his job at a nursery in northern San Diego County carrying three gallons of water and two bags of groceries. When he reached the canyon where he lived in a makeshift hut, a white car drove past and someone shot an air rifle at him. When several teenagers got out of the car and started to follow him, Díaz dropped his bags and started running. Behind him, he could hear the boys taunt, "Go back to Mexico!" Before the night was over on July 5, 2000, Diaz and four other elderly migrant workers were shot with air rifles and beaten with rocks and metal pipes by eight high school students.

Just a hundred miles away from the canyon where Díaz lives, volunteers from San Diego set up water stations in the Anza-Borrego desert in an effort to help illegal border crossers survive their journey across the hot sands. Since the U.S. Immigration and Naturalization Service's Operation Gatekeeper has made it more difficult for illegal immigrants to cross the border in more settled areas, over one hundred border crossers a year die from dehydration in the remote deserts and mountains of California and Arizona. The volunteers carry gallons of water to remote locations throughout the desert and erect flags to mark the sites.

As the two examples above illustrate, Americans have a complex—and at times contradictory—attitude toward illegal immigrants. On the one hand, many Americans feel compassion for the people who risk their lives in dangerous border crossings. On the other hand, some people—sometimes the same people—demand stricter border policies that will keep illegal immigrants out.

Many analysts argue that the United States treats illegal immigrants unfairly. They assert that draconian immigration policies demonize illegal immigrants and foster a climate in which racism and scapegoating flourish. Immigrant advocates maintain that the boys who attacked Díaz probably felt that their actions were justified because the men were illegals (they weren't—all were legal residents). San Diego mayor Susan Golding said the attack "undermines the basic freedom that we all take for granted: the freedom to work hard and not be subject to attacks because of who we are."

Other commentators do not agree that the United States treats illegal immigrants unfairly. They believe that it is the United States—not the illegal immigrants—that gets scapegoated. Mexico is to blame for the deaths of Mexican nationals in U.S. deserts, they argue, because Mexico does not provide a decent living for its people. Doris Meissner, commissioner of the Immigration and Naturalization Service, defends Operation Gatekeeper. She contends that the immigrant deaths that result from it are "a major safety and humanitarian issue—no two ways about it. And obviously we want Mexico increasingly to take responsibility." Most important, immigration opponents argue that immigrants knowingly undertake the risk to come and are ultimately responsible for what happens to them.

Once in the United States, illegal immigrants will work with U.S. employees, rent from U.S. landlords, interact with U.S. citizens, and be subject to U.S. laws. In the following chapter, the authors debate whether or not the United States treats illegal immigrants fairly.

U.S. Border Agents Treat Illegal Immigrants Inhumanely

by Michael Huspek

About the author: *Michael Huspek is an associate professor of communication at California State University San Marcos.*

A recently concluded report by the San Diego office of the American Friends Service Committee (AFSC) reveals 267 complaints of human and civil rights violations suffered by persons at the hands of law enforcement officials in and around San Diego. While the complaints involve the Sheriff's Department in Vista, San Marcos and Fallbrook, the San Diego Police Department and the California Highway Patrol, those agencies most frequently singled out are U.S. Customs and the Immigration and Naturalization Service [INS], including the Border Patrol.

Tales of Abuse

Among the complaints are 63 narratives, recorded over a three-year period, that provide a uniquely human look at how law enforcement agencies may be operating on the edge of lawlessness. Among the complaints are: illegal stops and searches of persons and their private property; verbal, psychological and physical abuse; deprivation of food, water and medical attention; and use of excessive force.

The narratives represent a highly diverse population. This includes undocumented immigrants such as Jorge Soriano Bautista who, detected entering the United States without legal documentation, ran from the Border Patrol until he was hit hard in the back by an agent's Ford Bronco, knocking him to the ground and causing him to black out.

Upon regaining consciousness, Bautista heard his arm snap while being handcuffed, and he again blacked out. Bautista was given no medical attention for

Reprinted from "Law and Lawlessness in San Diego," by Michael Huspek, *San Diego Union-Tribune*, February 26, 1998. Reprinted with permission from the author.

either his broken arm or the blow to his body caused by the Bronco. Instead, he was hauled to the border and stuffed by agents back under the fence onto the Mexican side.

Many of the narratives are also voiced by legal residents and citizens of the United States. Consider Abel Arroyo, a 19-year-old U.S. citizen who attended the San Diego Regional Center for the Developmentally Disabled. Attempting to pass through the San Ysidro Port of Entry after a brief shopping trip to Tijuana, Arroyo declared his U.S. citizenship and showed his birth certificate, state ID and social security card.

INS agents refused to believe him, however. In fact, one of the agents taunted Arroyo, hurled racial insults at him and then punched him in the stomach. For seven hours he pleaded with officers to be allowed entry, but to no avail. Without identity documents, he then wandered the streets of Tijuana for days until he met a man who agreed to smuggle him across the border for a fee. Eleven days after being denied entry into his own country, Arroyo was smuggled across the border and reunited with his family.

Vows of Change

The INS has not been altogether oblivious to complaints such as these. In 1998, John Chase, head of the INS Office of Internal Audit (OIA), announced that public complaints to the INS had risen 29 percent from 1996, with the "vast majority" emanating from the southwest border region.

More than 2,300 complaints were filed in 1997 as opposed to the 1,813 complaints filed in 1996. An additional 400 reports of "minor misconduct" were placed in a new category that previously had not been used. Chase emphasized, however, that the 243 "serious" allegations of abuse and use of excessive force that could warrant criminal prosecution were down in 1997 as compared to the 328 in 1996. These "serious" cases are considered distinct from "less serious" complaints such as "verbal abuse, discrimination, extended detention without cause."

On the same day that Chase spoke to the public, the INS issued a spate of press releases detailing an action plan that is meant to increase the information being made available to the public, expand dialogue between INS and community groups, enhance dissemination of INS information, increase public knowledge about complaint procedures, improve complaint process case management and incorporate local community-based training of INS staff.

> ***"Those agencies most frequently singled out [for human rights violations] are U.S. Customs and the [INS], including the Border Patrol."***

Such changes are to be commended. Better training and monitoring of agents is sorely needed as they are being deployed in the field at an unprecedented rate. And with a steady rise in state funding, coupled with increasing points of contact between agents and the public, it is essential that the community have a better understanding of the application, logic and effects of law enforcement practices. Such measures, moreover, need to be implemented by U.S. Customs and all other law enforcement agencies, as well as the INS.

Border Agents Need to Be Held Accountable

Nevertheless, such proposed changes do not go far enough in the right direction. Most vitally needed is an external review board—with genuine citizen participatory input—that can objectively determine the validity of complaints. This need is patent in light of the track records of the two offices most responsible for dealing with public complaints: the INS' OIA and the Office of the U.S. Attorney of the Southern District.

Complaints appear to be routinely swept under the carpet within the OIA. And the U.S. Attorney's Office does no better. Of the 63 AFSC-assisted complaints filed at different times over the 1995–1997 period, all received back an identical form letter stating: "After careful review . . . we have concluded that there is insufficient evidence to establish a prosecutable violation of the federal criminal civil rights statutes."

Beyond institution of an external review board, further discussion needs to be devoted to the frequency and nature of abuses being committed by law enforcement personnel. Given that virtually all of the complaints in the AFSC study are voiced by persons of Hispanic descent, a most obvious inference is that law enforcement in the southwest region is being applied discriminatorily.

This is not to state that all law-enforcement practices are racially motivated; nor is it to claim that all agents who engage in such practices are driven by racist sentiments. Yet the number and frequency of complaints are enough to suggest that law enforcement practices are being applied discriminatorily.

The current process of distinguishing "serious" abuses such as rapes or shootings from "less serious" abuses is inadequate. Verbal abuse, discrimination and extended detention without cause must be treated as the crimes that they are. What distinguishes the verbal abuse that frequently accompanies excessive use of force by law enforcement officials from hate crimes?

In an atmosphere where immigrant strawberry pickers have been sighted between the cross-hairs of an intensified criminalization strategy, it seems fitting that law enforcement officials' violations of the law also be treated as crimes and not merely as forms of institutional misconduct.

We grant to our law enforcement agencies an enormous responsibility, including the right to authoritatively intervene into our lives. There are boundaries that cannot be transgressed, however. The law is not to be enforced arbitrarily; nor is it to be enforced selectively against some but not others. Above all, law enforcement officials cannot abrogate subjects' human and civil rights. To do so constitutes a breaking of the law that instills terror in us all.

U.S. Growers Take Unfair Advantage of Illegal Farm Workers

by T. Alexander Aleinikoff

About the author: *T. Alexander Aleinikoff is a senior associate at the Carnegie Endowment for International Peace.*

Who harvested the fruits, vegetables, and nuts that graced our Thanksgiving tables? Most Americans, taking a moment to think, would know that immigrant labor in American fields brought in this autumn's crop. The circumstances of these workers' lives, however, are less well-known. The stark reality is that more than half of all farm workers live below the poverty line and the vast majority have no health insurance. And despite a general economic boom and increases in industry productivity and revenues, the real wages of farm workers have continued to fall—as they have for the past 20 years.

Invisible Workers

The people who work in the fields tend to be invisible participants in American society, and often by their own preference: The overwhelming number of farm workers are migrants, many of whom are in the United States unlawfully.

While conditions in the fields have attracted the attention of neither the public nor the political candidates in the 2000 election cycle, important new legislation backed by major growers has recently been introduced in Congress. The pending legislation, now in the Senate, attempts to deal with problems that have bedeviled American agriculture and policy makers for years. It would seek to guarantee growers a stable foreign work force by easing wage, housing, and recruitment requirements in existing law regulating guest-worker programs. It would also provide an "earned amnesty," in which green cards are offered to illegal workers who toil in the fields for the next five years.

The debate over farm-labor policy has been polarized for years; there is, in

Reprinted from "The Green Card Solution," by T. Alexander Aleinikoff, *The American Prospect,* December 20, 1999. Reprinted with permission.

fact, little chance that a political compromise will be reached before the 2000 elections [the legislation was still pending at press time]. The result is not an unhappy one for the public at large. American consumers pay a smaller part of their income for food than consumers in virtually all other developed countries. But if, as former Texas governor George W. Bush has reminded us, it is unfair to balance the federal budget on the backs of the poor, isn't it unfair to balance family food budgets on the backs of immigrant workers?

Laborers in the Fields

The primary cause of the bleak economic situation of farm workers is a dramatic oversupply of labor, fueled by high levels of undocumented foreign workers. Conservative estimates are that 50 percent of the seasonal agricultural work force is undocumented. That number probably rises to about 70 percent during harvest time. Huge increases in federal resources for border control have not noticeably stemmed the flow of undocumented workers, and Immigration and Naturalization Service (INS) enforcement efforts have for years given growers a virtual free pass. Recognizing the ready availability of undocumented labor, a 1997 General Accounting Office (GAO) report concluded that "[a] widespread farm labor shortage does not appear to exist now and is unlikely in the near future."

U.S. immigration law provides an avenue for the importation of legal temporary agricultural workers. The H-2A program, named for a subsection of the immigration code, has been on the books since 1986, with earlier versions dating back decades. But only a tiny proportion of immigrant farm workers arrive in the United States as H-2A workers. In 1998 about 35,000 of these guest workers were admitted, out of a peak farm work force of more than a million. (The majority enter the United States to work in the tobacco fields of North Carolina. Other H-2A workers pick apples and other fruits in the Northeast; some herd sheep.)

The reason for the relatively small number of temporary guest workers is obvious. Why should growers in the Southwest use a cumbersome federal program (which includes wage, transportation, and housing guarantees) when a plentiful supply of undocumented workers is readily at hand? Perhaps a serious federal enforcement effort in the fields could drive the growers to seek legal H-2A workers, but huge increases in federal resources in the past six years have largely gone to the border, not to interior enforcement. And the INS knows how to take a hint. When the INS raided the Vidalia onion fields in Georgia a year ago, members of Congress let the agency know that its efforts to stem illegal immigration had gone too far. The GAO re-

"The stark reality is that more than half of all farm workers live below the poverty line and the vast majority have no health insurance."

ported in 1996 that less than 5 percent of 4,600 INS investigations completed that year involved employers in agricultural production or services. While the government has not released more recent data, nothing suggests that enforcement levels have increased.

The situation, according to the growers, is changing. They argue that border enforcement is beginning to have an impact, and that even a few raids on fields can create significant concern because of the risk that the INS—somewhat like a tornado or a flash flood—could destroy a harvest with a well-timed enforcement action. More significantly, growers are receiving notifications from the Social Security Administration (SSA) telling them that many—sometimes most—of the Social Security numbers that they have submitted for their workers do not appear to be valid. The SSA reports are a part of a program intended to ensure the proper recording of Social Security contributions, not to enforce the immigration laws. But attorneys now tell growers that if they have "constructive knowledge" of illegal employment, they may be liable for penalties under immigration law.

"The primary cause of the bleak economic situation of farm workers is a dramatic oversupply of labor, fueled by high levels of undocumented foreign workers."

While there is no current shortage of workers, growers are forecasting increased disruptions in the flow of labor down the road. Their current legislative proposal is an attempt to be prepared.

Legislative Stirrings

In earlier years, growers have asked for expansive temporary-worker programs that would permit the entry of large numbers of farm workers during harvest time. Opposition to such plans by the Clinton administration and farm-worker groups have led growers to adopt a more nuanced approach this time around. Front and center in the new legislation is a proposal to offer legal status to much of the undocumented farm labor force. The idea is that a legalization strategy can satisfy growers by creating a stable work force while also appealing to farm-worker groups.

Under the bill, foreign workers who have worked in agriculture for 150 days in the past year would be able to apply for a temporary legal status. If they remain in agriculture for five years, working at least 180 days each year, they will be eligible for green cards (technically, "permanent resident status"). It is estimated that a legalization program along these lines would bring legal status to perhaps 400,000 laborers, roughly half the undocumented farm workers currently estimated to be residing in the United States.

This would stabilize the work force. Workers with temporary status are likely to stay in the fields because their green cards depend on five years of agricultural labor. But growers argue that modifications in the H-2A program are needed as well, given the industry's need for large numbers of short-term workers at harvest time. (They further contend that in the long term, an expanded guest-worker program will be necessary once the legalized workers get their green cards and seek work outside agriculture.) The legislative package would make the H-2A program more favorable to growers by softening the formula for setting wages, permitting growers to meet housing requirements by paying a housing allowance, and changing procedures for testing domestic labor markets before foreign workers could be brought in. Growers have sought to make these changes politically palatable by extending the weakened H-2A protections to more farm workers—even those who are not part of the H-2A program.

Farm-worker groups have strenuously criticized the industry's proposals. They object to the legalization proposal as "indentured servitude" and assail the proposed weakening of standards in the H-2A program. They call for more effective enforcement of existing labor laws and for unionization.

The thrust and parry here are familiar. While all parties agree that the status quo is unacceptable, the two sides talk past each other. Farm-worker groups, invoking the legacy of Cesar Chavez, are essentially conducting a human rights campaign; the industry is talking about global competitiveness and the role of agriculture as one of this nation's leading export sectors. These perspectives admit little common ground. But might responsible policy makers find acceptable solutions?

"Indentured Servitude"

The growers' goal of a stable, legal work force is appropriate, but it is not enough. The issue is how to achieve that goal in a way that moves toward relieving the staggering poverty of the largely alien work force that picks America's crops.

Workers' standard of living is directly tied to the wages and hours agricultural industries offer. Poverty results from low wages combined with chronic underemployment: Most farm workers average less than 30 weeks of work a year, at wages not much above—and sometimes below—minimum wage. The math here is easy, if dismal.

> ***"There is no persuasive evidence that providing a living wage to farm workers will put U.S. producers at a competitive disadvantage."***

On the wage side, advocates argue for better enforcement of existing laws. They point to Department of Labor surveys showing significant violations of minimum wage rules (a 1998 study found that 20 percent of surveyed California raisin growers did not pay minimum wage). Furthermore, the federal minimum wage only applies to employers whose employees work at least 500 "man days" per quarter, a standard that may exclude as many as half of seasonal workers. Piece-rate systems common for some tasks may also produce wages below the minimum hourly wage.

But it is not clear that either extending or enforcing the minimum wage is the answer to farm-worker poverty. Whether or not the minimum-wage law applies to a particular grower, it appears from the data that the prevailing wage for most farm workers is, on average, at or above the minimum wage. To make progress, wages would have to be raised substantially.

Growers argue that wage increases are ultimately counterproductive because U.S. goods are now competing in a world market. Higher labor costs, they contend, will price American goods out of the market and thus undermine farm-worker employment. The industry's arguments are common ones in this era of globalization. But there is no persuasive evidence that providing a living wage to farm workers will put U.S. producers at a competitive disadvantage. Indeed, agriculture's experience under the North American Free Trade Agreement suggests the contrary. A recent report from the Department of Agriculture shows a significant increase in fruit and vegetable exports to Mexico (as well as a substantial increase in imports from Mexico) in recent years. It thus appears that the higher wage scales for U.S. workers do not place U.S. goods at a competitive disadvantage—even in Mexico. Furthermore, even substantial increases in wages will produce only minimal increases in retail prices. This is so because wages paid to farm workers constitute a relatively small portion of the final retail price of agricultural products.

> ***"Given the ready availability of false documents . . . a grower who complies with the law may nonetheless have a labor force that is predominantly illegal."***

But action on wages can only go so far in an industry where there is not enough work for available workers. The key, it would appear, would be regulation of the supply of labor, which in this industry would mean effective enforcement of immigration laws. But neither growers nor farm-worker advocates support this option.

The growers' need for labor is highly seasonal and time sensitive. Enhanced INS enforcement would present a serious problem because it would threaten the removal of a large percentage of the work force at crucial times. Growers argue that they ought not be held responsible for an illegal work force because under the law they are entitled to hire workers with papers that appear to be valid. Given the ready availability of false documents that meet this test, a grower who complies with the law may nonetheless have a labor force that is predominantly illegal.

Farm-worker groups aren't in favor of increased INS vigilance, either. They argue that the costs of enforcement ought not to fall squarely on the workers who, despite a lack of status, have been performing labor that is highly valued (if underpaid).

Farm-worker advocates urge legalization as a preferred strategy. Legal status, the argument goes, gives workers the security to demand higher wages and better conditions, to complain to authorities about abuses, and to unionize. Growers, for different reasons, have signed on to a legalization proposal. The "earned amnesty" program in the pending legislation would provide a stable and legal work force—one that would not be disrupted by INS enforcement actions.

> ***"Legalization [of illegal farm workers] on the grower's terms only reinforces grower power over workers."***

A legalization program might seem like a pipe dream in the current political climate, but anti-immigrant trends did not prevent Congress from enacting legalization provisions for tens of thousands of Central Americans and Haitians in 1997 and 1998. While any proposal for a blanket amnesty for undocumented workers may be beyond the political pale, programs aimed at particular groups may well succeed.

The problem in reaching agreement here is that growers and farm-worker advocates seek legalization programs that are fundamentally incompatible. Growers want to ensure that aliens granted status will stay in the fields—this accounts for their proposal that green cards will be available only to workers who work more than 180 days a year in agriculture for five years. Advocates seek immediate status in order to shift bargaining power and improve conditions. They argue that legalization on the growers' terms only reinforces grower power over workers, who will depend upon the good graces of employers to furnish them with work over many years in order to secure full legal status. Although grower representatives bristle at their opponents' use of the phrase "indentured servitude," it's not hard to see how the power dynamics would work. The grower proposal would provide an almost captive labor force for an unconscionable period of time. Furthermore, the requirement of 180 days of labor per year exceeds the number of days worked by a significant portion of the undocumented work force; so the growers' proposal would ultimately leave perhaps hundreds of thousands of farm workers currently in the United States without permanent legal status.

A Possible Compromise

Despite widespread agreement that the status quo is not acceptable, there is no agreement about what should be done and thus little likelihood that legislation will be enacted before 2000. Advocates will not accept the legalization scheme presently contemplated by growers, but growers are unlikely to propose anything that cannot guarantee them a stable work force. And there will be no agreement on what should happen to the H-2A program, although it is possible that growers will be able to muscle through Congress some minor concessions. At that point, both sides may be able to declare victory—advocates because they have prevented a new temporary-worker program, growers because they have prevented any untoward changes in their wage structure—and they will go home and wait for the results of the 2000 elections. Meanwhile, hundreds of thousands of farm workers will continue to live in illegal status, working for wages that most American workers would not accept for themselves.

If both sides are willing to move from their well-entrenched positions, it is possible that a legislative compromise could be crafted. A legalization proposal should be the main focus—if it can lead to a steady workforce for growers and better wages and conditions for workers.

A workable plan might be to grant green cards off the bat, conditioned upon continued work in agriculture for a short period of time. The immigration law uses this approach in other areas. An investor who sinks $1 million into a U.S. enterprise that creates 10 or more jobs is given a conditional green card. If the enterprise is still going two years later, the green card becomes permanent; if not, the investor is deportable. Similarly, alien spouses sponsored by citizens and immigrants get conditional permanent resident status. The conditional status is removed if the marriage survives for two years. By analogy, farm workers could be granted green cards, which they could use to find labor anywhere in agriculture. With the green card, they could sponsor close family relatives and be entitled to benefits and opportunities generally available to permanent residents. If they stay in farm work for two years, the conditional status should be removed. The legislation should also set the annual number of days of labor required at a level that most farm workers currently in the United States could meet.

"Hundreds of thousands of farm workers will continue to live in illegal status, working for wages that most American workers would not accept for themselves."

Because there is no shortage of farm workers, a legalization program for workers already in the fields should give growers the legal workforce they say they want. Under this plan, there would be no need for a new large-scale guest-worker program. Similarly, there would be no reason to weaken current H-2A protections—although steps still need to be taken to streamline the H-2A application process to ensure that short-term workers can be brought in during times of spot labor shortages.

Farm-worker advocates ought to be willing to see the plan as offering a status significantly better than "indentured servitude." Even if workers are committed to employment in the agricultural sector for two years, a green card provides important benefits as well as a sense of security.

The possession of legal status might or might not put upward pressure on wages. So long as there is a free flow of undocumented labor, wages are likely to stay low. Thus, an effective overall approach requires enhanced INS enforcement. The administration needs to foster discussions between growers and farm workers over what such an enforcement effort could look like. It should not include random raids on fields, which terrorize workers and disrupt production. Rather, once the legalization program is under way, the INS should conduct employer audits to identify workers who are not authorized to work. Employers could be directed to legal sources of labor—such as newly legalized workers. Reducing the supply of undocumented workers will have effects both on wages and on demand for legal workers, who will be more interested in jobs that pay better.

More serious enforcement of labor laws is also needed. Since 1986, Department of Labor wage and hour investigations in agriculture have been cut almost in half, despite the department's survey evidence that substantial minimum wage violations occur in the industry. There needs to be a commitment by Congress to increase enforcement funding and a commitment by the department to make agriculture a priority.

Another route to higher farm-worker incomes would be an increase in the Earned Income Tax Credit. This strategy may be more politically acceptable than direct action on the minimum wage because its impact comes in the form of reduced tax receipts (in a time of big surpluses) rather than higher prices at the supermarket.

Together, these measures will put upward pressure on farm-worker wages and reduce the oversupply of labor. The longer-term result may well be the substitution of capital for labor in the fields. Some observers say that U.S. agriculture is "on the cusp" of significant mechanization. It is the present abundance of farm workers that is the main impediment to wider use of machines, according to some experts.

Would mechanization be desirable? The prime example here is the Florida sugar cane industry, which for years imported H-2A workers. In the late 1980s, several class action lawsuits were brought to enforce various provisions of H-2A contracts (including wage guarantees and transportation costs). Around the same time, the Department of Labor's tightened enforcement led to adverse publicity for the industry. Mechanical harvesters, which had been in use elsewhere for years, were improved for conditions in Florida. By 1995 the industry was completely mechanized. Today no cane cutters enter under the H-2A program. (And their capital investment has not put growers at a competitive disadvantage: In the past few years, Florida sugar cane crop yields per acre and overall production have increased—even as prices have fallen off a bit.)

Mechanization is an acceptable outcome when combined with a legalization program for current farm workers. Their green cards will give them access to the general economy as farm jobs decline. As the sugar cane example makes clear, mechanization will also undercut the need for large-scale temporary-worker programs.

The Power of Consumers

While a reasonable legislation package could be crafted, don't expect it to materialize before the current electoral cycle has run its course. This unhappy conclusion suggests that solutions may lie more in the hands of American consumers than in Washington.

To date, consumers have been conveniently absent from the debate, increasingly conscious of the benefits of a healthy diet, and benefiting from low fruit and vegetable prices but blissfully unaware of the conditions under which crops are produced. What is needed is a public education campaign that brings the basic facts before the American public. Such efforts have increased awareness about sweatshops in the United States; students have successfully protested the sale of college merchandise produced overseas under substandard working conditions.

The Clinton administration could sponsor the development of a core set of labor standards, relating to wages, housing, safety, and sanitation. An energized public could demand that supermarkets not buy produce from growers who cannot certify that they meet the standards. The result might be a slight rise in the price of produce. But it is a fair guess that Americans would be willing to pay a bit more for fruits and vegetables to improve the lives of the hundreds of thousands of farm workers and their families who provide America's bountiful harvest while living below the poverty line.

Border Fatalities: The Human Costs of a Militarized Border

by American Friends Service Committee

About the author: *American Friends Service Committee is a Quaker organization that works to promote social justice. Its arm—the Immigration Law Enforcement Monitoring Project (ILEMP)—monitors the effects of immigration control policies at the southern border.*

For nearly a decade, the Immigration Law Enforcement Monitoring Project (ILEMP) of the American Friends Service Committee (AFSC) has documented the heavy costs of immigration control policies at our country's southern border. Over the years, ILEMP has demonstrated beyond question a widespread and persistent pattern of abuses of civil and *human rights* by immigration authorities, ranging from verbal assaults, to illegal detention, to homicide, and falling on native-born as well as immigrants.

In 1996, a study published by the Center for Immigration Research at the University of Houston, and sponsored by ILEMP, sheds new light on the bitter human costs of current border control measures. The study, entitled "Migrant Deaths at the Texas-Mexico Border, 1985–1994," reveals that hundreds of border crossers die each year, casualties of the risks that undocumented migrants routinely take to evade immigration authorities.

The study adds a sobering new voice to our national dialogue on immigration—at a time when policy makers from across the political spectrum seem bent on imposing ever harsher and more militaristic conditions on those who cross the border. Bills currently pending before both houses of Congress, as well as recent moves by the Immigration and Naturalization Service (INS), all promise a dramatic upsurge in border control efforts. Yet such a response, as the University of Houston researchers warn us, will most likely only increase the human toll, "forc[ing] migrants to move to more dangerous terrain or take greater risks to avoid apprehension."

Reprinted from "Border Fatalities: The Human Costs of a Militarized Border," by American Friends Service Committee, 1996. Reprinted with permission.

What Does the University of Houston Study Tell Us?

- A minimum of 190, and, more likely, as many as 330 people die every year while attempting to make undocumented crossings into Texas. Some two-thirds of these fatalities are a result of drownings in the Rio Grande. (Texas accounts for roughly half of the 2,000-mile-long border between Mexico and the United States.)
- Evidence exists that a substantial majority of migrant deaths are never officially registered in vital statistics data bases. The University of Houston researchers compared official Texas vital statistics for 1993 and 1994 with administrative logs from local fire departments (which respond to reports of drowning victims sighted along the river). During that period, 56 fatalities attributed to migrants were registered in state vital statistics records, while 136 were recorded in administrative logs—a discrepancy of 240 percent.
- Of those deaths that are officially registered, as many as half of those who die are never identified. On the U.S. side of the border, the lack of resources for properly identifying bodies and determining the cause of death contributes to this problem. The study documents how in most counties, official procedures are rarely followed, leading to over-hasty burials and cursory attempts to locate family members. (Identification rates are substantially greater on the Mexican side and in El Paso, the one Texas jurisdiction where a Medical Examiner must determine the cause of death.)

"Policy makers from across the political spectrum seem bent on imposing ever harsher and more militaristic conditions on those who cross the border."

- Prejudice is also undoubtedly a factor. The study quotes one local Justice of the Peace as saying that "if a judge has reason to think that a body is from this side, it's a good idea to order an autopsy. If it's from the other side . . ." Likewise, an informant for one media account is quoted as stating that when local officials "find them in the river, they just assume it's death by drowning, and it's just another illegal Mexican. They're not from here. They don't matter. There's no investigation. There's no questions. But it's still a human being, isn't it?"
- The fatalities that are analyzed in this study may just be the tip of the iceberg. In every instance, the University of Houston researchers used conservative assumptions to estimate numbers of deaths, in order to guard against unduly inflated figures. Using their conservative methods, 21 deaths were attributed to railway accidents for the ten-year period covered by the study. Yet the Federal Railroad Administration (FRA) reports 382 fatalities to trespassers on trains in the state of Texas for the same ten-year period, and FRA and railway officials believe that many of those who died in this way were undocumented migrants.
- Likewise, nearly all of the deaths reported in the study occurred near popula-

tion centers along the border. This may reflect a tendency by undocumented migrants to move along major highways and transportation routes—or it may indicate that additional deaths in isolated areas are going unrecorded.

- In concluding their study, the University of Houston researchers state: "Death among undocumented migrants at the border constitutes a public health problem of nontrivial proportions. It is, however, a problem that especially affects the citizens of one country (Mexico), while the policies that affect the health risks are set by the government of another country (the United States). Further, on the U.S. side of the border, those responsible for monitoring the severity of the mortality problem are local and state officials. These officials have no direct say in the policies of border enforcement that give rise to the deaths."

> ***"Death among undocumented migrants at the border constitutes a public health problem of nontrivial proportions."***

Increasing the Risk of Violence and Abuse

The University of Houston study appears at a time when Congress seems poised to dramatically worsen a border enforcement environment that is already prone to violence and abuse. The "Immigration in the National Interest Act" (HR 2202, sponsored by Rep. Lamar Smith) would effect the most drastic changes in our immigration laws in more than 70 years. Its Senate counterpart, the "Immigration Reform Act of 1996" (S 1394/S 269, sponsored by Sen. Alan Simpson), is only slightly less ambitious. These bills follow on sweeping reform legislation passed in 1986 and 1990, enacted with the stated purpose of "shutting the door" to immigrants who enter illegally in search of work.[1]

We believe that this legislation is fundamentally misguided, in that it does not respond to the actual causes of immigration. Like its predecessors in 1986 and 1990, the new legislation purports to be the instrument through which undocumented labor migration at last will be curtailed. Yet like its predecessors, it makes not one passing reference to the two major forces driving people to the desperate step of attempting illegal entry into this country: the terror of war and the crushing burden of joblessness and economic dislocation.

Indeed, one might well question whether undocumented immigration is the true target of border control policies. Although only 40 percent of undocumented immigrants enter the U.S. at the southern border, fully 88 percent of enforcement resources are concentrated there. Even the INS acknowledges that at least half of undocumented immigration occurs away from the border, and involves not illegal entries, but people who enter with valid tourist visas and stay past their expiration.

1. The Immigration Reform Act was passed in 1996. The Immigration in the National Interest Act (HR 2202) was also passed in 1996.

Likewise, Mexicans make up a minority (39 percent) of undocumented immigrants in the United States, but an overwhelming majority (90 percent) of those arrested for "illegal" immigration. From this perspective, the intensification of enforcement at the southern border may be seen more as an expression of resistance to the *social* integration of Mexico and the United States, whose populations have been increasingly intermingled for more than 150 years, in an era when government policy on both sides is promoting an ever-increasing *economic* integration between our two neighboring countries.

INS agents in the field know that higher barriers in one place merely divert border crossers elsewhere. Terming such intensive crackdowns "squeezing the balloon," they acknowledge the futility of measures designed to make the crossing more difficult. One Border Patrol supervisor told a reporter that "if someone is determined to come across, they're going to make it. What's driving these people is human needs." Another explained why he and his colleagues did not bother to warn those they apprehended not to try to cross again: "You put yourself in their shoes, and you can see exactly what . . . is going on out here. You can understand where they're coming from." Another said simply: "Everybody has a right to work, to make a living, for his dignity. I assure you if the roles [of the countries] were reversed, I'd be in Mexico."

What Will Be the Impact of Impending Legislation?

The new legislation would heap armaments and fortifications on the border (including fourteen miles of triple fencing in the San Diego sector) and mandate vast increases in border guards (up to 4000 over four years). This legislation would strip the already powerless of the few constitutional protections they can now claim, and in myriad ways cut deeply into the civil and human rights of citizen and immigrant alike. People fleeing from persecution to request asylum at our borders would be forced to make their case at the gate or face summary denial; people who cross the border daily to work a few miles from their home would, if apprehended, be sent deep into the interior of Mexico to "deter" their crossing again; those caught making a third attempt to enter would automatically be jailed in this country for the offense.

> ***"Mexicans make up a minority (39 percent) of undocumented immigrants in the United States, but an overwhelming majority (90 percent) of those arrested for 'illegal' immigration."***

Residents of border communities in the U.S. and Mexico have raised their voices to protest the senseless militarization of their neighborhoods, the increasing intrusion of INS, military and police officers into their lives, the razor wire that scars the landscape and the body. To their surprise they have been joined in protesting some of these provisions by the border-keepers themselves. The INS has warned that it cannot possibly recruit and train qualified agents at the rate Congress has proposed—a rate that would double the size of the Border Patrol in four years. The INS has argued that it will be forced to promote unqualified agents to supervisory positions, further weakening what it acknowledges is already a deeply inadequate system of internal discipline and accountability. It also warns that the proposed three-tiered fencing near San Diego, the nation's busiest port of entry, poses a significantly increased danger of injury to its own agents as well as to border crossers.

What Is the INS Already Doing at the Southern Border?

Such initiatives do not reflect a policy shift so much as an intensification of existing trends in border enforcement. Since 1993 the INS has seen a 72 percent increase in budget; in 1996 its staff will increase by nearly 25 percent.

In 1993 and 1994, the INS instituted blockades, with new physical barriers and massive increases in the number of Border Patrol agents, at the busy crossings in El Paso, Nogales and San Diego. Agents have made increasing use of military hardware such as helicopters, night-vision scopes and motion detectors, and National Guard troops and U.S. military bases have been integrated into border control operations.

As spending on nearly all other federal departments is slashed, INS will receive another substantial increase in funding in this election year, and has begun a major new initiative to further concentrate resources along the border. Under the new "Southwest Border Enhancement," more agents will be diverted from the Canadian border and interior sectors to patrol the border with Mexico. For the first time, local police will work directly with Border Patrol to transport and process immigrants.

> ***"U.S. lawmakers seek to fix the blame for . . . problems [caused by globalization] on immigrants, particularly Mexicans."***

AFSC's long-standing work monitoring abuses by immigration authorities leads us to believe that this "enhancement" of untrained personnel will greatly increase the incidence of civil and human rights violations at the border. Police departments in border communities will cease to be able to function effectively to protect public safety when immigrant communities identify them with the Border Patrol. Future studies of violence at the border, we fear, may well show an intensification of human suffering as a result of these measures.

The border has always been a treacherous place. But in the years 1995 and 1996, as border enforcement efforts of the Clinton administration have accelerated, the character of physical barriers at portions of the Mexico–U.S. border has changed dramatically, from chain-link fences to razor-edged steel walls, from relatively level ground to hazardous complexes of artificial embankments.

These barriers pose a greatly increased risk of injury for the people who must navigate them, whether migrants or border guards. In addition, to the extent that people are deterred from crossing at ports of entry, they are merely forced to attempt more hazardous methods of getting across. Some wade through heavily polluted rivers and swamps hoping the Border Patrol will not follow, sometimes standing immersed for hours trying to outwait agents on dry ground. Cars crammed past capacity with migrants drive through highway checkpoints at high speed and are frequently chased, resulting in injury and death. Those traveling on foot face hazards ranging from dehydration in the burning Arizona desert to brush fires in the mountains near San Diego.

Many migrants are venturing farther from traditional crossing-points into more isolated and rugged terrain, where they face much greater risks of injury and death. With the institution of blockade operations at the most heavily trafficked crossing points, more remote areas have seen an astronomical rise in attempted crossings and apprehensions. Far out in the desert migrants face a lack of shelter, food and water, and greater vulnerability to the "*coyotes*" or smugglers to whom they must entrust their lives. Border Patrol agents also face increased risks: one young agent fell to his death in the San Diego mountains last year.

Some Points for Consideration

Because these policies do not take the root causes of undocumented immigration into account, we believe that they are essentially unworkable, unlikely in the extreme to achieve their stated goal of "sealing the border." As the University of Houston researchers remind us, "previous research has shown relatively little effect of border enforcement on the volume of migration flows." Unwilling or unable to address the complex of problems in both countries presented by the unregulated globalization of the economy—among them joblessness, a persistent decline in real wages and standards of living, and weakening labor protections—U.S. lawmakers seek to fix the blame for these problems on immigrants, particularly Mexicans, and to take punitive and "decisive" steps to satisfy the public furor they have in large part created. In the process, border crossers and all immigrants are vilified as "illegals," perpetuating the myth that they are a drain on our society's resources and creating a climate in which they are seen as a fitting target for discrimination and violence.

In contrast to this dehumanizing discourse, the University of Houston study leads us to look at the human dimension of the border. Each fatality is a human life lost. Each hastily buried, unidentified body belongs to a family that waits, and wonders, and never knows. This burden of loss and grief is part of the cost of U.S. border control policies—although, as the University of Houston researchers remind us, it is a cost that is seldom considered, because it is not borne by those who set the policies. A more dispassionate, humane, and rational view of border enforcement policies would consider threats to human life as risks to public welfare that need to be reduced, not amplified.

In our decades of program experience along the Mexico–U.S. Border, as well as with migrants and refugees from many nations around the world, AFSC has thought long and carefully about our understanding of the place of borders in relations between nations. Our core vision is not of a world without borders, but of one where borders are the product of mutual agreement and are mutually acknowledged, jointly administered, and demilitarized. We believe that the legitimate interests of all parties can best be addressed through streamlined border crossing procedures that respect human dignity and rights. We note that economic and political decision makers are seeking to remove all limits to the international movement of capital, while placing increasingly harsh restrictions on the movement of people.

In closing, looking beyond our concern for the humanity of all border crossers, we must reiterate our conviction that current developments at the border have very troubling implications for the country as a whole. The blurring of lines among local police forces, immigration authorities and the military is a significant step in a very dangerous direction. The "worker verification" system in HR 2202 is tantamount to a national ID card, representing a break with long-standing and deeply held tradition in the United States. In these and other developments, we can see how attempts to sharpen the divide between citizens and non-citizens diminish the very concept of citizenship for all of us.

The Border Patrol Is Unfairly Blamed for Violence Against Illegal Immigrants

by Ken Hamblin

About the author: *Ken Hamblin is a syndicated columnist.*

In May 1997, in Redford, Texas, an 18-year-old Mexican-American teenager was shot and killed by a squad of Marines after he opened fire on them with a .22-caliber rifle.

According to the U.S. Border Patrol, local high-school student Ezequiel Hernandez Jr.—who certainly was old enough to know better—shot at four Marines who were watching a suspected drug-trafficking route.

Hernandez fired twice, the *Associated Press* reports, and was preparing to fire a third time when a Marine returned fire, striking him in the chest.

Relatives of Hernandez claimed he had taken his .22-caliber rifle to tend the family's 30 goats after dinner. They insisted they heard only a single shot, estimated to be about a half-mile away.

"Even if he did shoot at them twice like they said, I think they had no right to kill him," Hernandez's 26-year-old sister said.

Predictably, the Hernandez shooting has brought sharp criticism from immigrant-rights groups, who argue that using military troops along our porous southern border only incites violence.

And I predict that it won't be long before Ezequiel Hernandez is transmuted into the next Mexican-American martyr in a fanatical battle by fringe revolutionaries to deliver the Southwest back into the hands of Mexican sovereignty.

Meanwhile, to the best of my knowledge, nobody's asking the obvious question of why an 18-year-old Mexican-American goat herder would seek to pick a gunfight with U.S. Marines posted on the border.

For the life of me, I can't tell you what kind of logic this boy might have possessed.

But I am willing to wager that a rising incidence of U.S. Border Patrol agents being fired on by snipers had a lot to do with those Marines firing back at Hernandez.

As recently as May 19, 1997, the *Associated Press* reported that "a U.S. Border Patrol agent was released from the hospital . . . a day after he was wounded by gunfire from across the Mexican border.

"The agent . . . was alone in a marked Border Patrol vehicle near the border crossing," the report continued, "when someone in a car on Mexico's Ensenada Highway fired six to 10 bullets. Two pierced the windshield and grazed his head and shoulder. A third struck the hood of the Ford Bronco."

U.S. officials claimed the attack was unprovoked.

No matter how hard immigrant activists try to portray a one-sided attack on olive-skinned innocents, two-way gunplay between Border Patrol agents and Mexican banditos and drug dealers is not new.

In 1995, after a shootout between a Mexican border gang and federal agents near El Paso, a Border Patrol agent stationed in McAllen, Texas, told the *Washington Times:* "It's become more like a war zone out there."

The agent noted that this shootout had been only one of several cross-border incidents.

The problems stem from a new breed of Mexican criminal bent on looting slow-moving freight trains and confronting border guards.

"It's not just the common person coming over to find work anymore," one Border Patrol agent said.

"No matter how hard immigrant activists try to portray a one-sided attack on olive-skinned innocents, two-way gunplay between Border Patrol agents and Mexican banditos . . . is not new."

Let the liberal Polyannas romanticize the Mexican campesino all they like. The fact is that it is the successors of the Mexican bandito who have now chosen to up the ante by looting our trains, attacking American motorists and taking pot shots at our Border Patrol agents and soldiers.

Like I said, I can't tell you what motivated an 18-year-old Mexican-American to fire on a group of Marines.

I can tell you this, though: I'd rather report the death of an inept young sniper than the demise of a U.S. Leatherneck doing his duty.

Mexico Is to Blame for the Deaths of Illegal Immigrants

by Samuel Francis

About the author: *Samuel Francis is a nationally syndicated columnist.*

Like hurricanes and sex in the Oval Office, illegal immigration is something that everybody is still against. Yet—again like hurricanes and presidential sex—illegal immigration keeps happening. In 1998, despite vastly improved border security on the American side, arrests of illegals in San Diego alone are expected to exceed 200,000. But while almost all American politicians support tougher controls, their Mexican counterparts are openly refusing to take any measures to reduce the flow.

In September 1998, the *New York Times* reported that the head of Mexico's migration service simply refuses to do anything to discourage his fellow countrymen from violating U.S. laws and international agreements by moving north. "At no time will we take any action that could discourage Mexicans from emigrating to the United States," pronounced the official, Fernando Solis Camara. "That is because these are people who leave their families and their homes with the legitimate goal of bettering their lives."

Mexico's Callousness Causes Mexicans' Deaths

His remarks betray a good deal about the Mexican government and its aims that Americans, politicians or not, need to think about. In the first place, it tells us that Mexico actually wants its own population to invade the United States—partly to get rid of what it considers excess people, partly because it regards (at least unofficially) the southwestern United States as still Mexican, and partly because, as Mexican leaders have openly stated in the past, Mexicans in this country can build a fifth column that the compadres in Mexico City can manipulate to their advantage.

Reprinted from "Mexico Willing to Let Immigrants Die," by Samuel Francis, *Conservative Chronicle,* September 23, 1998. Reprinted with permission from Knight Ridder/Tribune Information Services.

But Mexico's refusal to staunch its own demographic overflow tells us something else as well: The Mexican government really doesn't much care about its own people or their welfare. Mr. Solis' remark was uttered in the context of a relatively new dispute over border security. As U.S. border security improves, illegals are driven away from the areas where they used to enter this country into more remote and more dangerous areas, with the result that more and more of them are being discovered—dead.

In California alone, more than 90 Mexican immigrants have been found dead in 1998. They get lost in the desert and die of thirst and exposure. Or they put their trust in smugglers, who simply abandon them as soon as they rake off their money. A new agreement between Mexico and the United States requires each country to place signs that are supposed to warn immigrants against trying to cross the border in certain areas. The United States has in fact placed more than 100 such signs.

Yet champions of unrestricted immigration in this country whine that the immigrant deaths are all the fault of the United States. If we hadn't increased security at the borders, they argue, then not so many immigrants would try crossing in dangerous places and fewer would die. That argument, of course, ignores the reality that the immigrants are violating our laws. If they don't want to die or risk death, maybe they should stay home.

Mexico Should Help Control the Border

And if the Mexican government gave a plugged peso for the well being of its own people, it would fire Mr. Solis and seriously try to discourage its own people from coming. Doing so might even help improve relations with the United States, whose people would then not be acquiring the sneaking suspicion that the Mexicans think most gringos in the Southwest ought to pack up and go back to Plymouth Rock.

But the Mexican government not only does not fire Mr. Solis; it backs him up. The Mexican consul general in Los Angeles tells the *Times* that the Mexican Constitution gives Mexicans the right to move where they want. and that includes other peoples' countries. Besides, he beams, "Here in the U.S., there also are laws that give the Border Patrol the responsibility to prevent people without documents from entering the country."

> ***"Mexico's refusal even to try to stop the exodus of its own population ought to tell us that it has no concern whatsoever . . . with the welfare of its own people."***

It's nice the consul general acknowledges the right of the U.S. government to do that, but of course we couldn't expect a little cooperation from him or his government, could we? As long as we can't, and as long as Mexico openly refuses to take any measures to stop the flow of illegals, the United States is perfectly justified in solving the problem the most effective way it can.

Mexico's refusal even to try to stop the exodus of its own population ought to tell us that it has no concern whatsoever either with the welfare of its own people or with respecting the laws and interests of its northern neighbor. As long as that's the case, our government should stop pretending that our neighbor to the south is a friend or an ally and start considering whether it may be an enemy whose real purpose is simply to conquer our land by tolerating, if not actually encouraging, its occupation.

Mexican Smugglers Are to Blame for the Inhumane Treatment of Illegal Immigrants

by Timothy W. Maier and Sean Paige

About the authors: *Timothy W. Maier and Sean Paige write for* Insight *magazine.*

Undercover agents in Texas smashed a family-led smuggling ring on July 13, 1999 that for 15 years specialized in sneaking thousands of illegal aliens past Border Patrol checkpoints in the Rio Grande Valley—sometimes disguising them as fans caravaning to high-school football championships.

On July 26, 1999, the U.S. Coast Guard called off the search for 40 Haitians missing when two smuggling boats went to the sharks between Florida and the Bahamas, resulting in "the most deaths in a smuggling case that I can remember," according to one Coast Guard officer.

On July 27, 1999, prosecutors in Florida won prison terms for six men convicted of running a sex-slavery ring in which Mexican women were lured to the United States with promises of opportunity and then forced to work off their transport fees in brothels.

Illegal Immigrant Express

Each of these cases marks an unscheduled stop on an international underground railroad—call it the Illegal Immigrant Express—that in spite of such derailments still manages to deliver more than a million riders a year to destinations in the United States with a reliability and efficiency that puts Amtrak to shame. And all of this is pulled by an engine, well-oiled by high demand and huge profits, that seems to pick up steam despite the best efforts of U.S. immigration agencies to sidetrack it.

"Here the trafficking in human beings is bigger than the drug business," says border-town mayor Ray Borane of Douglas, Ariz., whose constituents are being overrun since crackdowns in Texas and California have moved the action into their backyards. "It's more lucrative, there's little risk for the smugglers and the United States keeps giving them their cargo back."

Lucrative Trade

Borane says he would like the Mexican government to intervene before the tense situation in Douglas "gets too far out of hand" but doubts it will happen. "There's so much money involved that nobody in Mexico wants to see it stopped," he tells *Insight.*

Though it still is poor by U.S. standards and in places verges on the squalid, a drive through Agua Prieta, Mexico, just across the fence from Douglas, suggests the town is enjoying a boom—one that nobody on either side of the line credits to the North American Free Trade Agreement. New construction is everywhere. Many homes compare favorably with those found north of the fence. Shiny late-model cars and pickups cruise the streets. The town's side streets bustle, especially around the hotels and guest houses that cater to migrants awaiting their ride on the underground railroad. During the height of smuggling season, the town's population doubles, and that's good for the local economy. "This people-smuggling business has surpassed narcotrafficking here," Agua Prieta Mayor Vicente Teran Uribe recently told the *Arizona Daily Star,* "and the Border Patrol strategy is the reason."

"Mexican women were lured to the United States with promises of opportunity and then forced to work off their transport fees in brothels."

"The more physical difficulties and Border Patrol agents there are, the greater the need for people to resort to and rely on smugglers," says University of Notre Dame sociology professor Jorge Bustamante, noting the ironic symbiosis between Border Patrol agents and the smugglers they hunt.

In 1994, immigrant smuggling along the Arizona line was an ad hoc activity conducted by individual opportunists, costing as little as $200 for those who bothered to hire a guide, ace *Daily Star* border reporter Ignacio Ibarra wrote in a recent exposé on the smuggling rings. But in 1999 the short trip from Agua Prieta to Phoenix can cost an illegal as much as $1,500—$9,000 or more if they come from Central America—Ibarra reports, generating big profits.

Sophisticated and Violent

"It's becoming a numbers business, even more than it has been," a Border Patrol source in Arizona confirms to *Insight.* "And down here they're getting very violent. We've had guides kill each other over groups."

Though the evolution of alien trafficking may have been anticipated by the Border Patrol, the speed with which the smuggling networks have grown and their increasing technical sophistication have taken agents by surprise. Yet, bust by bust, law-enforcement officials are piecing together a better picture of their highly organized internal structures and the complexity of their operations.

Bisbee, Ariz., police have detained more than 800 vehicles carrying some 5,000 illegal aliens in 1999 alone, according to the *Daily Star*. And documents recovered in the vehicles lend credence to the suspicion that these are not fly-by-night operations. "There's too much of this going on for it to be a coincidence," Bisbee Police Sgt. Bill Bagby says. "This isn't just a few people getting together to buy a car—this is racketeering." U.S. attorneys agree and are employing federal money-laundering and antiracketeering laws to go after smuggling groups.

Another telling indicator of the highly organized structure of the smuggling rings is their increasing use of specialists to move their human contraband. "Coyote" still remains the catchall term for smugglers along the Mexican border, but there are subspecialists. *Polleros* (rough translation: chicken wranglers) specialize in recruiting and rounding up clients. *Brincadores* (rough translation: fence-hoppers) are locals who guide clients across the border. Then there are "scouts," who monitor Border Patrol movements from area perches, often with a slingshot handy for pelting their passing trucks.

> ***"Because the penalties for participation are nominal and the rewards are relatively great, it's not difficult for smuggling networks to recruit border-area youths to abet traffic [in illegal immigrants]."***

Because the penalties for participation are nominal and the rewards are relatively great, it's not difficult for smuggling networks to recruit border-area youths to abet the traffic, Ibarra reports. They easily mix in with their own contraband, in spite of Border Patrol efforts to separate the chicken wranglers from the chickens, though sometimes their expensive boots and clothing give them away. The Mexican government doesn't consider these migrations illegal, so little effort is made to enforce the country's relatively harsh laws against trafficking in people.

Altruism or Cruelty?

Smugglers say that they are providing a valuable service. "They're going to cross anyway," a coyote recently said of the aliens. "Imagine how many people would get hurt or die if they couldn't count on my help."

But such altruism tends to end abruptly when things go badly. Aliens, finding themselves abandoned by their coyotes, often turn themselves in rather than die in the desert. But others aren't so lucky—there were 254 alien deaths along the Mexican border in 1998, many of them occurring when guides misled, abandoned or endangered their charges.

Although one wouldn't know it walking the boomtowns of the Mexican border or talking with Border Patrol agents in Arizona who wrestle constantly with futility, a recent study by Syracuse University nonetheless indicates a dramatic escalation in the government's battle against illegal immigration.

> ***"The aliens are held, sometimes for long periods of time, and occasionally in a hostagelike situation, until family or contacts in the United States pay the balance owed."***

Prosecutions of illegal aliens jumped from 7,335 in 1992 to 14,616 in 1998, court records show. As a result, Immigration and Naturalization Service [INS] convictions were the second highest, behind only the FBI, among all federal law-enforcement agencies. Though the bulk of the prosecutions still occur along the U.S. border with Mexico, San Diego no longer is the epicenter of the INS' criminal-enforcement activities. Prosecutions there have declined 37 percent since 1992, as the strict Operation Gatekeeper has pushed smugglers eastward. In Arizona and San Antonio, Texas, on the other hand, prosecutions have jumped to nearly five times what they were in 1992.

The study reports that the "sharp increase in all enforcement was the result of decisions during the last few years by the Clinton administration and Congress dramatically to increase the size of the INS, to toughen selected immigration laws and push federal prosecutors to pay more attention to the subject." INS personnel were increased from 17,368 in 1992 to 29,420 in 1998.

"Bill Clinton deserves credit for taking the lead, but the amount of resources allocated to programs to combat alien smuggling is woefully inadequate," says Roy Godson, president of the National Strategy Information Center and a professor at Georgetown University, who frequently has testified before Congress on this issue. "Congress also bears some responsibility. They have not adequately addressed the problem."

Hard to Measure, Hard to Solve

Most experts think the available numbers aren't necessarily a good measure of whether administration polices are reducing the total number of illegal aliens entering the United States. The optimistic numbers do not say who is being busted, whether small-time border hoppers or big-time operators. And they contradict anecdotal evidence that the underground railroad is steaming right along.

In 1996 the INS estimated that some 5 million undocumented immigrants were residing in the United States, with about 250,000 more added each year. Other estimates peg the number of illegals who annually enter the country at 1.5 million. And even though there were some 172,312 illegal immigrants expelled in 1998, compared with just 42,471 in 1993, this barely puts a dent in the problem.

"We mostly deal with the tail end of the problem," acknowledges Barry Tang, assistant district director for INS in Baltimore. Though a long way from the borderlands, even Tang's experience suggests to him that the problem is escalating. In 1999 his agents arrested 19 Mexican illegals who flew on a USAirways flight from Pittsburgh to Baltimore. A few months earlier, 46 illegals were arrested at Chestertown Foods Inc., a chicken-processing plant on Maryland's eastern shore.

In most of the Maryland cases, organized crime does not seem to have been involved, Tang says. Mostly the rings are run by labor contractors looking to profit by supplying U.S. companies with the low-wage workers they crave. The area companies that benefit usually are mom-and-pop shops, Tang says.

Operation Figaro

Providing a revealing glimpse inside the murky underworld of immigrant smuggling is Operation Figaro, in which agents of the INS infiltrated a Central American alien-smuggling ring, resulting in the May 1999 indictments of 17 individuals in Phoenix. With the cooperation of suspects snared in a bust of Phoenix stash houses (where aliens are held pending their next move through the pipeline), INS agents for several months set themselves up in the smuggling business, culling a windfall of intelligence about how such organizations conduct business.

According to Jack Weaver, supervisory special agent with the INS in Phoenix, the process begins with the recruitment of prospects in the cities of Central America. After paying half of the base fee of around $5,000, with the balance due upon delivery in the United States, the groups are escorted north through Mexico, bribing their way past police and military checkpoints along the way.

The human cargo is guided over the border at Douglas—crossing repeatedly if necessary—before being driven by back roads to Phoenix, which "has got to be the people-smuggling capital of the world," according to Weaver. There the aliens are held, sometimes for long periods of time, and occasionally in a hostagelike situation, until family or contacts in the United States pay the balance owed. In one episode observed by INS, two aliens were held by smugglers for 30 days while their families scrambled to scrape together enough to free them. This resulted in charges of hostage-taking being brought against smugglers in a unique application of federal antiterrorism statutes.

"Smuggling groups are fighting to get control of the pipeline or stealing aliens from each other."

Depending on their final destination, the aliens then are driven typically to Las Vegas or Los Angeles, again staying clear of interstates, where they are provided (for an extra charge) with counterfeit documentation and put on outbound flights. Acting on occasional tips from airline ticket agents, such flights sometimes are boarded by INS agents at their final destinations.

At the height of Operation Figaro, 50 to 100 Central Americans a week were passing through the three INS stash houses, according to Weaver—a mill kept grinding by the steady stream of people moving through the pipeline and the string of contractual obligations and bribes that bind network conspirators together. And although this particular smuggling ring was relatively humane in treatment of its charges, says Weaver, "we've had cases of people holding guns to children in front of their parents to get their money."

Growing Violence Amongst Smugglers

As with their drug-running counterparts, violence sometimes flares between rival gangs of alien traffickers due to double-crosses, "load stealing" and territorial disputes. "There's been some shooting here in Phoenix, when smuggling groups are fighting to get control of the pipeline or stealing aliens from each other," Weaver tells *Insight.*

"Certainly the level of violence has grown here in Phoenix among smugglers in the last two or three years," Weaver says. "We had one instance not too long ago when two people were shot up outside a drop house," using the smuggler's weapon of choice, a Chinese-made SKS. "And just the other night the police here arrested some guys with an SKS getting ready to go and hit a house. Some of it is, 'You didn't pay me.' Some of it is to rub out the competition."

Guide-on-guide violence also occasionally occurs. At the Aqua Prieta headquarters of Grupo Beta, a Mexican police force charged with protecting immigrants from being victimized by smugglers, *Insight* was shown photos of one guide believed to have been shot in the face by a rival.

Despite the intelligence learned during Operation Figaro, much of the alien-trafficking world remains terra incognito even to those who study it closely. But an academic who requests anonymity due to his ongoing work in the field says that while it's definitely a huge, profitable, transnational industry, he has "not seen evidence that there's some Mr. Big behind it." Of course you have to distinguish, he adds, between those rings that traffic in Mexicans and those that smuggle non-Mexicans, because the latter group is by necessity more sophisticated and well-organized.

An International Problem

Mexicans still make up the vast majority of apprehensions along the southern border, but in recent years agents have noted an upswing in the number of OTMs, or "Other-Than-Mexicans," who get reeled in with the catch. In addition to many Central and South Americans, the Border Patrol's Tucson and Yuma sectors have in 1998 and 1999 also apprehended 119 mainland Chinese, 31 Bulgarians, 15 Cubans, 10 Lebanese, 10 Poles, nine Filipinos, nine Indians, seven Iranians, six Romanians and six Russians. And other stations along the border have apprehended Canadians, Yugoslavs, Vietnamese, Egyptians, Czechs, Lithuanians, Iraqis, Israelis, Syrians, Laotians and one unlucky chap from Burkina Fasso.

Baltimore's Tang says that to be smuggled from Asian countries such as China can cost $20,000 to $30,000 for illegal passage. In some cases, aliens must pay off the fees at such a high interest rate that they become virtual slaves to their smugglers.

Though some law-enforcement officials stubbornly view immigrant smuggling as a victimless crime, "Unfortunately, the reality is that migrants are often subjected to inhumane or dangerous treatment and, in the case of Chinese, to extreme forms of violence," according to Jonathan Winer, deputy assistant secretary of state for narcotics matters and law enforcement. In 1996 smugglers in Seattle kidnapped three children they had transported to the United States, demanding money from their parents in China. Before the three were freed, one of the girls repeatedly was raped. The same smuggling group kidnapped a Chinese businessman and two women in New York. The case ended with the businessman shot in the head but alive. A finger of one of the women was cut off and the other was assaulted sexually and lost several fingers.

"Migrants are often subjected to inhumane or dangerous treatment [at the hands of smugglers]."

Chinese smuggling rings earn as much as $3.5 billion annually, according to U.N. estimates. Between 1993 to 1996, the Coast Guard recovered 2,100 Chinese smuggled aboard 11 ships. They were lucky. Sometimes smugglers have been known to toss their human cargo to the sharks, destroying evidence of illegal activity, Winer notes.

Law Enforcement Successes

But the INS is fighting back and has had its victories against the networks. More recently those efforts have been bolstered by the FBI, which didn't involve itself in alien-smuggling cases before 1997, when a memorandum of understanding between the Border Patrol and FBI inaugurated a new era of cooperation.

One result of the teaming has been Rio Stop, a two-year undercover operation that busted 12 members of a family-led ring involved in alien-trafficking for 15 years. The family owned two apartment complexes, a motel and a house that provided squalid staging grounds for transporting people past INS checkpoints in the Rio Grande Valley. Authorities began to investigate the Contreras family in January 1997, when more than 350 undocumented immigrants were found, packed like sardines, into a Raymondville, Texas, apartment complex.

Other notable successes include:

• In May 1995, federal agents charged five people running three houses of prostitution in the Los Angeles area. The prostitutes were Mexican women who had been recruited by the smuggling organization in Acapulco, Mexico. As in the recent Florida case, the women were promised jobs as housekeepers but were made to engage in prostitution to pay off their smuggling fees.

• In August 1995, INS agents charged nine members of a smuggling ring that transported Mexicans across the border to a drop house in San Diego. Vehicles disguised as plant-nursery delivery trucks hid cages in which aliens were transported, generating weekly profits of about $100,000.

• In March 1996, a three-month INS probe in Mexico City, Houston and McAllen, Texas, resulted in the breakup of the Global Smuggling Ring. The mission ended in arrests of 15 smugglers, including the ringleader, who remains in federal custody. The gang had operated for seven years and specialized in smuggling Chinese, Indian and Pakistani nationals who paid as much as $28,000. They used air, bus and van transportation to move the illegals through Russia, where entry visas for Nicaragua were obtained.

There is little doubt that the smuggling organizations involved are huge. "You can't repeatedly beat the Border Patrol and U.S. Customs Service without a sophisticated organization; you're talking about a multibillion-dollar-a-year industry here," says Godson. He estimates that "well over half of illegal immigration or alien smuggling involves organized crime."

For now, few solutions are on the table. Godson laments, "The Clinton administration and Congress have not requested anything more to be done. And that's a shame, because the illegal migration affects the quality of life in the United States."

Chapter 4

How Should Government Respond to Illegal Immigration?

Chapter Preface

Fauziya Kasinga left her native land of Togo for the United States in order to avoid female genital mutilation (FGM)—a traditional practice in her culture in which a woman's clitoris is cut away in order to deaden sexual pleasure. Detained for entering the United States illegally, Kasinga spent two years in jail before being granted political asylum by the Board of Immigration Appeals in 1996.

Prior to Kasinga's case, immigration law had granted asylum to members of any "particular social group" which was being persecuted by its government, but the law did not consider women to constitute such a group. The Kasinga ruling changed that by defining women as a "particular social group" and by including in the legal definition of "persecution" such acts against women as FGM. Few in the United States condone such treatment of women, yet many are concerned that opening up U.S. asylum to all persecuted women will open the floodgates to thousands of illegal immigrants.

Since its founding, the United States has opened its doors to refugees, promising them a better life. In 1951, the United States established a formal political asylum policy in response to a United Nations statute that forbid nations from returning anyone to a country in which his or her freedom would be in danger. In subsequent decades, however, increasing numbers of illegal immigrants requesting asylum began arriving on U.S. soil, and lawmakers began to modify the policy to limit who could come, how many, and by what criteria their individual cases would be judged. In spite of increasing restrictions, however, the Immigration and Naturalization Service continues to grant asylum to thousands of illegal immigrants a year.

As the number of asylum seekers has risen, the debate over who should be granted asylum has grown more heated. Those who favor liberal asylum policies argue that the United States is a symbol of freedom and justice and has an obligation to help people throughout the world who are fleeing oppressive governments. Geraldine Brooks, author of *Nine Parts of Desire: The Hidden World of Islamic Women*, argues that granting asylum to persecuted women sends the message that Americans "hold certain things sacred—and among them are liberty, equality, the pursuit of happiness and the right to hold one's own beliefs."

Those against generous asylum policies maintain that such policies have created a "back door" for circumventing the regular immigration process. Opponents argue that granting asylum to too many illegal immigrants is unfair to legal immigrants who sometimes must wait years for admittance. In addition, as the Federation for American Immigration Reform (FAIR) reports, applications for asylum "have soared to 60,000 a year, with many claims frivolous or fraudulent."

Chapter 4

While asylum proponents argue that the United States should provide a safe home for women like Kasinga, others contend that the country already has more asylum-seekers awaiting a hearing than it can assimilate. At issue is the amount of responsibility the United States should bear for the misfortune of others. The authors in the following chapter debate how government should respond to illegal immigration.

New Restrictions Placed on Asylum Seekers Should Be Removed

by Michele R. Pistone

About the author: *Michele R. Pistone is an advocacy fellow at the Center for Applied Legal Studies at Georgetown University Law Center.*

Human lives are being put in danger by the 1996 Immigration Reform and Immigrant Responsibility Act. The new law contradicts America's tradition of offering a safe haven to people fleeing persecution by failing to accommodate the unique and often tragic circumstances that confront those seeking asylum.

Sensationalized Portrayal of Asylum Law

The most damaging portion of the 1996 law is the one-year filing deadline. Many genuine asylum seekers will not be able to meet the deadline because of the circumstances they face, including the trauma of torture, the threat of death, and fear for family members who remain in their home country.

The 1996 changes were based on a sensationalized and misleading portrayal of U.S. asylum law. Only about 17,000 people are granted asylum in the United States each year. Administrative reforms by the Immigration and Naturalization Service in 1995 closed the major loopholes that existed at the time, making the 1996 legislative changes at best unnecessary.

A Refuge for Oppressed People

Throughout its history, the United States has been a refuge for oppressed peoples from around the world. The Pilgrims, the Quakers, the Amish, and countless others came to these shores in centuries past, while in the more recent past immigrants have been Cubans, Jews, Southeast Asians, and others. What those diverse people shared was a belief that America could offer them refuge from government oppression.

Reprinted from "New Asylum Laws: Undermining an American Ideal," by Michele R. Pistone, *Policy Analysis,* March 24, 1998. Reprinted with permission from the Cato Institute.

Many people worldwide today face similar oppression; they live under governments that forbid them to freely exercise rights that Americans hold dear as fundamental freedoms and persecute them when they try. We grant political asylum to such persons: as a nation, we believe that government oppression because of one's race, religion, political opinion, nationality, or social group is wrong. Oppression undermines our fundamental values. Thus, we traditionally have granted sanctuary to victims of human rights abuses from around the world.

Through its refugee and asylum protection policies, the United States has always been at the forefront of protection issues, serving as a leader in garnering international attention and responses to refugee and humanitarian emergencies around the world. America's example has great influence on how other countries respond to refugees.

Notwithstanding this grand tradition of leadership in refugee protection, portions of a law passed by Congress, the Illegal Immigration Reform and Immigrant Responsibility Act of 1996 (IIRIRA), impose procedural hurdles that in many cases may prevent genuine victims of persecution from attaining asylum. The intention of the law was to reduce abuses, both real and perceived, in the asylum system, even though key reforms had already been made by the Immigration and Naturalization Service. If the new law does curb abuse, it does so only at the price of cutting down on all claims for asylum—without distinguishing between the valid and the fraudulent. It could damage one of America's noblest ideals, being a safe haven for those fleeing repressive governments.

The Nature of Governments

Americans know and are concerned that governments around the world oppress their citizens. We condemn the persecution of Christians and other religious minorities in Sudan, Cuba, China, Pakistan, North Korea, and countries that were part of the Soviet Union. We criticize the People's Republic of China's systematic repression of religious practices and study by the Tibetan and Uigher peoples. We cringe when we see the suffering of women and children refugees in Somalia and Rwanda, the mass graves in Bosnia, and the persecution of the Kurds in Iraq. We are outraged by the Chinese government's silencing of the student democracy movement in Tiananmen Square and the forced abortion and sterilization of Chinese people who want more than one child. And we denounce the practice of genital mutilation of young girls in Africa and the Middle East. We see images of human suffering on the evening news, read about the horrors of human rights abuses daily in newspapers, and wonder how all that could be happening and what we could do to help.

> ***"Let us not end America's ideal of offering a haven to the world's oppressed."***

Yet, despite our commitment to encouraging basic freedoms of speech, political opinion, and religion, IIRIRA has imposed restrictions on the ability of victims of such human rights abuses to escape government-sanctioned oppression and persecution and to seek refuge in the United States. . . .

Maintain the American Tradition

The current anti-immigrant trend should not be permitted to diminish the valued role of the United States as a haven for democracy and fundamental freedom. Since before America's founding, people have fled to this land to escape persecution by their governments at home. Whether from England, Germany, Russia, or Africa, refugees recognize that the U.S. government acknowledges and respects their right to believe what they believe and to be who they are, free from oppression.

In keeping with America's tradition, every effort should be made to lessen the random impact of the new laws on genuine victims of human rights abuses. That can be achieved in the short term by including safeguards to protect genuine asylum seekers in the asylum and expedited removal processes. The safeguards would be designed to prevent the return of genuine victims of human rights abuses to countries where they would face persecution, torture, or death. In the long term, the utility of the provisions should be revisited. Let us not end America's ideal of offering a haven to the world's oppressed.

The Government Should Not Increase Asylum Opportunities for Illegal Immigrants

by Ben J. Seeley

About the author: *Ben J. Seeley is executive director of the Border Solution Task Force, an organization that works for immigration reform.*

The old cliche "The road to disaster is too often paved with good intentions" could not be more applicable than it is to a provision included in the immigration Control and Financial Responsibility Act of 1996.

In a slick backroom deal, with the aid of a slick lobbyist, the Christian Coalition's national leadership and a ton of foreign campaign contributions, Title VI, Subtitle A, Refugees, Parole and Asylum was included in the 1996 act and voted into law.

A Pandora's Box

This provision, in essence, loosens the political asylum floodgates to economically impoverished immigrants waiting to flee their nations under the guise of single-child-per-family limitations or coercive birth controls.

Put more succinctly, this opens a proverbial "Pandora's box" for massive illegal immigration to the U.S. while encouraging fraudulent claims for political asylum from seriously overcrowded nations like China and India.

As a matter of fact, 36 Chinese who illegally entered the United States in 1994 have recently been released from the Immigration and Naturalization Service (INS) detention and are now awaiting disposition of their claims of political persecution under the coercive population control subsection of Title VI. It has been reported that all of these are probably unmarried males.

Reprinted from "Political Asylum Law Opens Floodgates," by Ben J. Seeley, *North County Times,* June 1, 1997.

Easy Entrance into the United States

There are those open-border enthusiasts who rejoice in the flimsy 1996 immigration legislation and still others who have acquiesced and now maintain that it was at least a step in the right direction.

Was it really? These same folks might not feel so smug if they were to face the fact that this provision almost begs poverty-stricken people from all over the world to jump on the "first thing smoking" and make way for the good old U.S. of A.

No longer will desperate Chinese smuggled in from mainland China cost the unscrupulous businessman $30,000 apiece to be stuffed into the hole of a rusty old freighter and end up in servitude for years. With political asylum claims virtually unchallengeable, the trip can be accomplished relatively cheaply as a visitor or student via airplane, luxury liner or simply as a crew member intent on jumping ship in the first U.S. port.

Once the prospective asylum claimant sets foot on U.S. soil or enters its territorial waters, all one has to do is say two words in English, "political asylum" and then await a refugee status determination. The basis for the request, of course, will be a claim that they are fleeing a repressive foreign regime because it practices coercive birth-control policies.

> ***"[Increasing asylum opportunities] opens a proverbial 'Pandora's box' for massive illegal immigration to the U.S. while encouraging fraudulent claims for political asylum."***

It will matter little whether or not that is their real reason. How can the INS possibly look into their minds? Furthermore, many seeking asylum for humanitarian reasons will travel through one or more safe-haven, neutral countries making their way to the U.S. The case can then be made that once they reach a neutral safe haven, their continued trek to the U.S. then becomes a personal choice for economic opportunity reasons.

This, by any rational thinking, negates the legitimacy of their political asylum claim and should facilitate a quick denial and removal to their country of origin. The U.S. cannot possibly fulfill the economic aspirations of the entire Third World and maintain First World conditions for its own citizens and legal residents.

Special Interests and Betrayal

Make no mistake about it, this political asylum provision is exactly what the 1996 act promotes, and for the most part, the lion's share of credit must go to the Christian Coalition national leadership for getting this self-flagellation provision voted into law.

For those who are bewildered and feel sold out by this provision, especially those rank-and-file members of the Christian Coalition who have expressed sincere surprise and outrage, it is even more ponderable when considering that early in 1996, the U.S. Ninth Circuit Court, in a very rare ruling favoring conservative immigration policy, declared that fleeing countries because of family size restrictions and coercive birth control policies does not constitute legitimate grounds for being granted political asylum.

It was almost a foregone conclusion that the apologists defending this ominous provision were going to jump at the chance to downplay the concerns. They rushed to point out that this refugee status is no big deal since it is limited to a maximum of 1,000 immigrants annually.

This is the moment of truth where good intentions grind to a halt and the road to disaster takes on the form of a superhighway. Exactly what 1,000 will be granted this status? The numerical capacity quotas will not in any way limit the number of potential claimants. Once a refugee program is set in motion, those fleeing to the U.S. for political asylum are virtually never removed nor deported yet all are entitled to have their claims adjudicated via immigration hearings.

Policing the Policy Is Impossible

U.S. immigration history will substantiate the fact that once refugee status is made available to the immigrants fleeing a particular repressive country, deportations are unheard of. Those that are granted temporary legal alien status while awaiting political asylum determination simply disappear into society, leaving the INS not a clue as to where they are.

It is shameful how the genesis of U.S. Immigration policies based on practical experience have failed to teach our elected officials or the so-called experts that numerical limitations without the means of control do not, have not, and will not work.

Interior INS enforcement over the past few years to the present is virtually nonexistent; fraudulent documents are more plentiful than ever and the Clinton White House administration is not likely to allow the INS to get a hold on anything.

On a routine basis, one can expect political asylum refugees to continue to arrive in greater numbers the longer the program is in force, and, of course, the INS investigative and processing capabilities is destined to become an even larger logjam.

Beyond Carrying Capacity

Just add these expected new numbers onto the existing 5 million illegal aliens already patting their feet in expectation of another massive amnesty, plus the 3.5 million legal immigrants backlogged to be naturalized under family chain migration and it becomes unavoidably clear that the U.S. is in jeopardy. How can a nation that occupies only 6 percent of the Earth's land mass even begin to take on such an impossible task? Especially one that is taking in over 2.5 million immigrants, both legal and illegal right now.

The 105th Congress had better busy itself and immediately pass restrictive legislation that will put an end to political asylum refugee status on the basis of coercive birth control or single-child limitations from countries who in all practicality waited much too long but have now recognized the drastic need to slow its birth rates and reduce its population.

Most of the First World countries that learned this over 30 years ago are now being impacted by massive Third World migration and are desperately trying to protect their borders.

Getting into the U.S. for most people in the world is like winning the lottery. It doesn't require an overactive imagination to surmise that, with over 4.5 billion people throughout the world living in bleak conditions more destitute than those of Mexico, even just immigrating to Mexico would enhance their chances for better living conditions and economic opportunities.

The main thing that will keep this from happening is that the Mexican government isn't suffering from a serious case of heart enlargement and won't allow it to happen.

Its leaders, as any responsible sovereign nation's leaders should, are not about to place its citizens nor its economy in such a perilous position. How can anyone argue with that?

The Children of Illegal Immigrants Should Be Granted Citizenship

by Stephen Chapman

About the author: *Stephen Chapman is a syndicated columnist.*

Even as you read this, there are Mexican women at pay phones just across the border waiting to go into labor so they can call an American ambulance, walk into the United States, catch a ride to the nearest public hospital and proceed to give birth at public expense. At least that's how Ron Prince tells it. The reason, says the California activist, is simple: the baby automatically becomes an American citizen, entitled to all social welfare benefits, and the mother gains permanent immunity from deportation. Then she can bring in her husband and other children with full legal status, allowing them to further abuse our hospitality.

Policy Based on Mythology

The story is mostly a mix of mythology and addled reasoning, but it serves to dramatize a political cause. After organizing the successful campaign for Proposition 187 in 1994,[1] which barred public education and other services to illegal foreigners in California, Prince was circulating petitions to get another initiative on the ballot in November 1996. At the heart of it was an idea that has been gaining support among those who want to reduce or stop immigration: denying citizenship to children born in the United States to illegal immigrants.

The petition drive fell just short of the number needed to qualify for the ballot, but the issue is far from dead. In Congress, in fact, birthright citizenship, a bedrock national policy since 1866, may be the next major immigration battleground. Though not a part of the current broad and inhospitable rewrite of immigration law introduced by Senator Alan Simpson and Representative Lamar Smith, the issue has already come up in Congress. On December 13, 1996, two

1. Proposition 187 was overturned by a mediator in 2000.

House subcommittees held a hearing on Representative Brian Bilbray's proposed statute to bar citizenship to children born here if their parents are not citizens or resident legal aliens. Meanwhile, Representatives Elton Gallegly, a Republican, and Anthony Beilenson, a Democrat, both of California, have proposed bills to make the same change by constitutional amendment.[2]

The proposals address a longstanding gripe of those who want to curtail the influx of people from abroad. Peter Brimelow's polemical 1995 book, *Alien Nation*, which gained notoriety for urging that immigration be not only reduced but revamped to bolster the white population, expressed amazement that we let the children of lawbreakers become full-fledged American citizens because of a mere accident of birth. So did Yale professors Peter Schuck and Rogers Smith in their more scholarly and temperate 1985 volume, *Citizenship Without Consent*. The anti-immigration Federation for American Immigration Reform (FAIR) favors the change, and executive director Dan Stein finds that it gets raves from the radio call-in crowd. In the climate dramatized by the triumph of Proposition 187, the proposal can't be dismissed as farfetched.

Anti-citizenship Proposals Are Unconstitutional

There is something annoying about the spectacle of foreigners getting a valuable right by breaking our laws. But enacting a statute to abolish birthright citizenship for the offspring of illegal immigrants, as Bilbray recommends, would be far worse. To begin with, it is almost certainly unconstitutional. The Fourteenth Amendment, adopted to confer full citizenship on black Americans after the Civil War, leaves minimal room for interpretation when it says, "All persons born or naturalized in the United States, and subject to the jurisdiction thereof, are citizens of the United States and of the State wherein they reside." Bilbray finds a blessing for his measure in that middle phrase. Foreigners who come here without the knowledge or consent of the U.S. government, he argues, are not truly "subject to the jurisdiction thereof." Under the Supreme Court's reading, Congress has been allowed to exclude a few classes of U.S.-born people from access to citizenship—children of foreign diplomats, for example.

But minor exceptions are not likely to justify a major one. The Fourteenth Amendment merely codified a longstanding common law rule that nationality was almost invariably determined by birthplace. The Supreme Court held in 1898 that a child born in San Francisco of Chinese parents was automatically an American citizen—which his parents, thanks to the Chinese Exclusion Laws, could never become. The amendment, said the court, "has conferred no authority upon Congress to restrict the effect of birth, declared by the Constitution to constitute a sufficient and complete right to citizenship." Even Schuck, a law professor who spent an entire book arguing that Congress has the power claimed by Bilbray, admits that his is a minority opinion among legal scholars—and that it

2. No bills have passed denying citizenship to children born to illegal immigrants.

was implicitly rejected by the Supreme Court in a landmark 1982 case. Testifying before Congress in December 1996, he said that since writing his book he has come to the conclusion that the policy he prefers should be brought about only by constitutional amendment: "So far-reaching a change should not be adopted by a transient majority in Congress."

Illegal Immigrants Do Not Come for Citizenship

Putting the measure in the form of a constitutional amendment, however, doesn't fix its other flaws. Prince notes that 70 percent of the births in Los Angeles County's public hospitals are to women here illegally—which proves merely that there is an abundance of illegal immigrants already in the area. Brimelow cites a study which found that 15 percent of Hispanic new mothers in California-border hospitals cross the border just to give birth and that one-fourth of this group did it so the child would be a U.S. citizen. This suggests that for every Mexican mother who comes here to take advantage of birthright citizenship, there are sixteen who come for a different reason. And that says nothing about the men who are here illegally. California hosts an estimated 1.7 million undocumented foreigners, and they produce no more than 100,000 new births each year. The late Barbara Jordan chaired the federal Commission on Immigration Reform, which proposed a number of controversial steps to crack down on illegal immigration. But, at the December hearing, even Jordan testified that there is no evidence that many people come here mainly to get citizenship for their kids.

Besides, Prince's claims about the entitlements that come with bearing a child here are almost entirely fictitious. An illegal immigrant is not allowed to bring other family members to the U.S. just because one of her children is born here. Nor can she claim any legal right to stay. In terms of immigration status, says Ned Lynch, the former director of strategic planning at the Immigration and Naturalization Service (INS), "it doesn't get her anything." If she is picked up by the INS, she will typically be offered "voluntary departure"—a bus ticket across the border, in the case of Mexicans—and, if she refuses, she can expect to be deported. Her citizen children may remain if they can find a guardian to take them in, but most leave with their parents. Only in rare cases, when the children are nearing adulthood after living their entire lives in America, do immigration judges sometimes waive deportation for the parents.

> ***"For every Mexican mother who comes [to the United States] to take advantage of birthright citizenship, there are sixteen who come for a different reason."***

In practice, few of these parents are deported because few illegal immigrants are deported. Most who are apprehended accept voluntary departure—about a million people a year, compared to only about 50,000 who are formally expelled. But most of those who get into the country have little to worry about as long as they stay out of trouble. About 95 percent of the illegal foreigners snared by the authorities are caught at the border. So having a baby here just to stay in the U.S. would mean going to an awful lot of trouble to get something that most illegal immigrants already enjoy: the opportunity to remain indefinitely.

Creating a Permanent Underclass

Denying citizenship to such children would do nothing to combat illegal immigration because it would neither discourage illegal immigrants from coming nor make it any easier to catch and expel them. It would, however, create a new class of residents who, despite being born and living their entire lives here, are denied a full place in society, solely as punishment for the sins of their parents—much like the Turks and other foreigners in Germany, which doesn't provide for birthright citizenship. Defining "Germanness" by blood, not place of birth, it makes citizenship available almost exclusively to ethnic Germans, including many born abroad and far removed from any national connection. By this logic, Russians of distant German ancestry find it far easier to get citizenship than third-generation "foreigners" who have never set foot outside the country. These immigrants, who began arriving in the 1950s, constitute some 9 percent of Germany's population, but nearly all of them remain aliens. Denying citizenship to children born here to illegal immigrants would produce a similar pool of the legally disadvantaged in the United States, which until now has had an enviable record of assimilating newcomers. And not only would these children be barred from citizenship—so would all their descendants. "Without a birthright citizenship rule or another amnesty, these illegals, their children and their children's children will continue to be outsiders mired in an inferior and illegal status and deprived of the capacities of self-protection and self-advancement," Schuck testified at the hearing.

"Without a birthright citizenship rule or another amnesty, these illegals, their children and their children's children will continue to be outsiders."

Denying citizenship to the children of illegal immigrants would not ameliorate the problem it claims to address. In fact, it would more likely fulfill the worst fears of the anti-immigration forces—creating, out of people born within our borders, an unassimilable community of estranged aliens. It's hard to see how that could be an improvement on a policy that, by treating them as Americans, makes them Americans.

The Children of Illegal Immigrants Should Not Be Granted Citizenship

by Brian Bilbray

About the author: *Brian Bilbray is a congressional representative from California.*

In the debate surrounding strengthening our immigration laws in order to reduce illegal immigration, citizenship is a pivotal concept.

Its importance was underscored by adoption of a "citizenship plank" as part of the Republican Party platform in 1996. The plank closely resembles federal legislation that I introduced in Congress in 1995 to eliminate the automatic citizenship status currently granted to the children of illegal immigrants born in the United States.

Clear definition of who *is* a citizen and who is a *non-citizen* of the United States is the foundation upon which rests this country's national sovereignty. This is a debate I believe we can expect to revisit now that the Democratic National Convention is under way in Chicago in 1996.

The 14th Amendment to the Constitution states: "All persons born or naturalized in the United States and subject to the jurisdiction thereof are citizens of the United States." Clearly, those who have entered our country illegally do not meet this definition, as they do not recognize the authority of our borders or our laws. I introduced my legislation out of a desire to protect the rights and privileges of legal immigrants and citizens and to eliminate a powerful magnet for illegal immigration.

Our current practice of granting automatic citizenship to the children of illegal immigrants is just that—a practice which has no legal basis, and is the result of a misinterpretation of our laws. I believe this misinterpretation can be clarified through legislation. There are extensive precedents for Congress; authority

Reprinted from "Eliminating the US 'Citizenship' Magnet," by Brian Bilbray, *San Diego Union-Tribune,* August 29, 1996.

to change or grant citizenship status. For example, Congress has statutorily granted citizenship to various Indian tribes 12 times since 1870.

Although some of my colleagues in Congress advocate a constitutional amendment to correct the current misinterpretation of the 14th Amendment, it is my view that this would be superfluous. The fact is that the U.S. Supreme Court has never ruled whether the child of parents on U.S. soil illegally (i.e., not "subject to the jurisdiction" of the United States), should receive automatic citizenship under the Constitution. Of the approximately 10,800 amendments proposed in the last 200 years, only 17 have been ratified. It is clear that there are practical considerations as well as legal precedent for implementing this change statutorily.

We must also consider this issue from a perspective driven by our basic fairness as Americans. Our current practice is an insult to all legal aliens who observed our immigration laws and came to the United States through the proper legal channels.

"The practice of granting automatic citizenship has established a powerful lure, while at the same time undermining our own immigration laws by rewarding illegal behavior."

I do not blame young mothers for wanting to give their babies the option of a better life in America. However, the practice of granting automatic citizenship has established a powerful lure, while at the same time undermining our own immigration laws by rewarding illegal behavior.

According to California health officials, approximately 100,000 illegal immigrants a year give birth in state hospitals alone, at a cost of $300 million to taxpayers. These are resources which must be diverted from our citizens and legal residents.

A San Diego State University study of 400 illegal immigrants found that 41 percent received welfare payments at some point after delivering. A year later, 34 percent of the group remained on welfare. The irony of the whole situation is that automatic citizenship status acts as a magnet, and taxpayer benefits such as health, education and welfare encourage illegal immigrants to stay in this country, where they are legally prohibited from working to support themselves and their children.

No one wishes to be punitive—my legislation would not strip citizenship from naturalized immigrants or those children of illegal parents who already have been granted citizenship. These children and their parents are by no means our enemies, and I don't want to disparage the motives of those who wish to come to America. I only question the manner by which they arrive—legally or illegally—and how our laws treat them accordingly.

Along with the 49 Republicans and Democrats who support my legislation in the House, I wish merely to be corrective. It is our moral obligation to clarify who deserves the rights and privileges of U.S. citizenship and who does not.

Our country must operate under the guiding principles and application of the rule of law. Therefore, those who break our laws to enter our country—all motivations aside—do not automatically deserve the honor of U.S. citizenship.[1]

1. Bilbray's bill was defeated.

The Government Should Allow Open Immigration

by John Isbister

About the author: *John Isbister is an economics professor and provost at the University of California at Santa Cruz.*

Americans typically express their opinions about immigration with certainty and moral outrage. I would like to argue, however, that most Americans are in an ethically fraught position with respect to immigration. We have deeply held convictions about the equality of all people. At the same time, though, we use immigration policy to perpetuate a privileged lifestyle at the expense of foreigners. We are not prepared to abandon either this use of immigration policy or the ideology of equality. At the very least, therefore, our moral stance should be one of humility, not outrage. . . .

The moral validity of border controls is drawn into question if we believe in the moral equality of all human beings. If only Americans have moral standing, or if Americans are more worthy than non-Americans, we do not need to take into account the rights of others on an equal basis. If all people are equally valuable, however, a policy that favors one group at the expense of another—such as apartheid, Jim Crow laws [laws that systematically segregate and oppress African-Americans] or immigration controls—seems on its face to be invalid.

Moral worth is not the same as merit. As philosopher Gregory Vlastos stated, "It differs from every kind of merit, including moral merit, in respect to which there are vast inequalities among persons." People earn merit by their behavior, talent and skills and may be judged quite differently. They are equally worthy, however, simply by virtue of being human beings.

Philosophers have made many attempts to demonstrate the equal worth of all people. For the most part, though, those of us who believe in equality treat it as an assumption, an axiom, not something to be proved. The axiom of equal worth is at the core of the two most important statements of political philosophy in American history, the Declaration of Independence and the Gettysburg Address.

In the Declaration of Independence, Thomas Jefferson wrote, "We hold these Truths to be self-evident, that all Men are created equal." He did not argue the point; it was "self-evident." The importance of equality was that equal rights accrue to all people: "They are endowed by their Creator with certain unalienable Rights, that among these are Life, Liberty, and the Pursuit of Happiness."

Neither Jefferson nor his Virginian compatriots conducted their lives in accordance with these "Truths," for they were slaveholders. Similarly today, most people do not base their actions on a commitment to the equality of all people. Nevertheless, for the most part, we believe in equality not because we have reasoned it out and considered the arguments pro and con but because it is "self-evident."

The radical equality of the Declaration of Independence was restricted sharply by the more conservative Constitution of 1789, a document that, among other things, protected slavery. As Gary Wills has argued, however, Abraham Lincoln's Gettysburg Address of 1863 had the effect of subverting the Constitution by restoring equality as the central American value. It began, in words now as familiar to Americans as those of the Declaration, and more familiar than any in the Constitution, "Fourscore and seven years ago, our fathers brought forth upon this continent a new nation, conceived in liberty and dedicated to the proposition that all men are created equal."

Neither document says "all Americans are created equal." Jefferson and Lincoln may or may not have implied "people" by their use of the word "men," but in our current reading we do. These most formative of American documents assume the equality of all human beings.

People are equally valuable and therefore have equal rights. It does not follow from this that they have unlimited rights. Rights often conflict with one another, and when they do, the liberal state (that is, the state based on the presumption of equal worth) is justified in restricting some rights in order to protect others. Whenever it restricts rights, however, the state must be able to give morally justifiable reasons why it has done so—otherwise it forfeits its claim to liberalism and descends into despotism.

Immigration controls restrict free movement by establishing groups that have unequal rights. Among those people in the world who wish to live in the United States, the favored are allowed to, and others are not. Can one successfully argue that immigration controls that infringe on some people's liberties are justified because they protect more important rights and liberties? Or does their allocation of unequal rights to people who are of equal worth make them morally impermissible?

> ***"We use immigration policy to perpetuate a privileged lifestyle at the expense of foreigners."***

Freedom of movement is a facet of the "Liberty" that the Declaration of Independence takes to be an inherent right of equal human beings. Countries that systematically restrict the movement of their people are rightly criticized. In recent years, the clearest example of the morally unjustified restriction of internal movement was in South Africa, which enforced its apartheid system with pass laws.

As a mental exercise, one could ask how a law passed by the residents of New York City that restricted the permanent entry of Americans who were not city residents would be judged. Leaving aside the fact that it would be unconstitutional, would it be morally justified? The people of New York could offer some good reasons for the law. New York is already crowded and cannot tolerate further population growth, they might argue. The sanitation system is close to breaking down, the schools are crowded, the welfare system is bankrupt, the homeless shelters are inadequate and the unemployment rate is rising.

These sorts of arguments would not prove convincing to most Americans, who would find the restriction on personal freedom too onerous. Every day people migrate into (and out of) New York for compelling reasons. They move in order to accept jobs or to look for jobs or because their jobs have been relocated to New York. They could not have the same jobs in Boston or Chicago because New York is unique (as are Boston and Chicago). They move to New York to be with their families or to care for friends or for any number of other reasons. The decision to migrate to New York is seldom taken lightly; people have good reasons. The interests that New Yorkers have in restricting entry, although perhaps meritorious, are not of sufficient weight to permit such massive violations of the rights and interests of outsiders. New York cannot justify its own immigration policy, morally.

"The purpose and effect of American immigration controls are to maintain a state of inequality in the world between the haves . . . and the have-nots."

If this argument is accepted, how can one accept immigration restrictions in the United States? What makes the United States different from New York? Nothing much, except sovereign power. If New York were a sovereign state it might well have an immigration policy, notwithstanding the fact that the policy violated the rights of non-New Yorkers. New York's laws would not have to conform to the laws and constitution of a broader entity, so its government would not be compelled to take into account the rights of people outside its jurisdiction. This would not, however, make a restrictive immigration policy ethical, unless one could somehow argue that by virtue of their sovereignty New Yorkers abandoned their moral connections to people outside their border.

Reasoning by analogy, it is hard to find an ethical justification for the United States' restricting entry across its borders. In fact it is harder, since the people of the United States are privileged, vis-à-vis the rest of the world, in a way that the residents of New York are not, in comparison to other Americans. New

Yorkers could argue plausibly that among American cities their city is not so special, that people denied entry into it could find comparable amenities in other cities. The United States occupies a unique position in the world, however, or at least the long lines of potential immigrants would so indicate. The great majority of immigrants and potential immigrants hope to enjoy a significantly higher standard of living in the United States than they experienced in their home countries. Immigration controls on the U.S. border therefore restrict access to privilege.

"Border controls . . . automatically create a class of people in the United States who have fewer rights, the undocumented."

It is the protection of privilege that is so damaging, ethically, to the country's immigration laws. It makes U.S. border controls even less justifiable than New York's would be. The purpose and effect of American immigration controls are to maintain a state of inequality in the world between the haves (the Americans) and the have-nots (the foreigners, especially the potential immigrants). Americans maintain immigration laws because they fear that unrestricted entry would lead to a major influx of people, that the newcomers would compete for scarce resources and jobs in the United States and that they would drive down the standard of living of residents. No doubt it is in the interest of the privileged to protect their privileges, but it cannot be ethical if that protection has the effect of further disadvantaging the unprivileged.

The ethical case against immigration controls is based, therefore, not just on the fact that they convey unequal rights to morally equal people but that they do so in a particularly damaging way, so as to protect advantage and deepen disadvantage. To understand the importance of this, one can consider the argument that some types of unequal treatment are morally justified. For example, a system of preferential hiring in which race is taken into account treats different groups of people unequally, but it may be fair if it is designed to benefit people who have been exploited or to dismantle a system of racial injustice. Unequal treatment is clearly unjust, however, when it is used to perpetuate rather than break down a system of privilege and disadvantage. This is just what American immigration controls do. They violate the equal worth and equal rights of people in an egregious way, by sheltering already advantaged Americans at the expense of relatively disadvantaged potential immigrants.

A second ethical argument against border controls is that they automatically create a class of people in the United States who have fewer rights, the undocumented. The undocumented are branded as illegal; police forces arrest and deport them. Border controls will never eliminate this group, as long as foreigners who are denied entry see some advantage in being in the country. Undocumented immigrants are part of American society; they work, pay taxes, contribute to their communities and have personal relationships with American citizens and legal residents. Yet many rights that legal residents take for granted are denied to them. . . .

The very meaning of border controls is that some people are denied entry. The denial must be enforced if the border controls are to exist. Consequently, the undocumented must have rights that are inferior to those of other residents. The only way to avoid the unequal treatment of American residents is to remove the restrictions on immigration.

The Government Should Not Allow Open Immigration

by Garrett Hardin

About the author: *Garrett Hardin is professor emeritus of human ecology at the University of California, Santa Barbara.*

As the 20th century draws to a close, uninvited immigration has become a problem worldwide. Migration from poor or troubled countries to rich and relatively peaceful nations was always an intermittent fact of life, but few governments have seen it as a 'problem'. Most have just tried to hold the would-be immigrants at arm's length. Of the powerful nations, the newest one, the United States, is somewhat confused in its policy. . . .

The troubles of the present are rooted in the past. We need to understand how the compromises worked out early in the century produced difficulties in later years. Alone among the nations of the world, America boasts a Statue of Liberty. Within the base of the statue are displayed verses that welcome the immigrants—unconditionally. No other nation has adopted such a policy. (Deductions from these facts are left to the reader.) Inconsistently, the general populace at the beginning of the century indulged in a rich amalgam of uncomplimentary epithets for the migrants the statue supposedly welcomed in: Dagos, Wops, Sheenies, Polacks, Krauts, and many others.

Americans were not alone in speaking thus: it is a part of primitive human nature to distrust the stranger. There is even a word for this attitude: xenophobia, fear of foreigners or foreign things. Non-verbal animals show the same reaction. Over the eons of evolution and history, a congenital distrust of new acquaintances has no doubt been of survival value. For all species, distrust seems to be the default position in social interactions. Our biological nature places the burden of proof on any implications of trustworthiness.

Early in the century, opinion-leaders in some human societies started to oppose the default position of human conduct. The word *ethnocentrism* was coined in the year 1900; it was advanced toward popularity in 1907 by William Graham Sumner's *Folkways*. The dictionary defines this word as "belief in the superiority of one's own ethnic group." Whatever their eventual fate, most '-isms' are coined to condemn the named practice or attitude. Think of *racism, sexism,* and *ageism:* all potent condemnatory terms in our time. *Ethnocentrism* was also coined to condemn. This term helped shift the balance of public opinion away from distrust of immigrants. We are embarrassed now to think of the way our ancestors used to speak of Dagos, Wops and Krauts. More—and this is important—we have a tendency to infer that because the opposition to immigrants used to spring from ethnocentrism and xenophobia, any proposal made now to limit immigration must necessarily owe its origin to the same motives. This is not necessarily so. The historical development of U.S. immigration policy has been admirably summarized in *Mass Immigration and the National Interest* by Vernon M. Briggs, Jr., on which the following summary is based.

The 19th Century to 1914

There were few restrictions on immigration, other than barring entrance to known criminals, mental defectives and people with serious communicable disease. The beginning of the first World War brought this period to a close. But before it did, the stage play by Israel Zangwill in 1908 contributed a bit of rhetoric that still influences decisions: the title of his play, *The Melting Pot*. In it the author asserted that "America is God's crucible, the greatest melting pot where all the races of Europe are melting and re-forming." Note that Zangwill did not extend the idea of melting beyond the peoples of Europe. Within those restrictions, the ideal of loyalty to a single sovereignty was embraced by leaders among both hosts and immigrants. The official name of the change process was *assimilation*.

1924

In the "National Origins Act" Congress discriminated among applicants from different nations. Quotas were set, with 96 percent being assigned to European countries and 4 percent to various others. No limits were set on immigration from the Western hemisphere. Doors continued to be closed to Asiatics. The Chinese, barred since 1882, were not admitted until 1943; the Japanese, who had been officially denied admission in 1908, were not admitted again until 1952. (Remember that in World War II, which lasted until 1945, China was an ally, Japan an enemy.)

1940

The legal control of immigration was transferred from the Department of Labor to the Department of Justice. Paralleling this organizational change, as time went on the effects of immigration on employment and labor were often denied or ignored, while the effects of immigrants on crime (including drug-dealing) were emphasized. An increasing number of economists maintained there was no "hard evidence" that immigrants took jobs away from natives, hence there was no need to be concerned about the effects of immigration on labor. (Anyway, criminal activities, whether of immigrants or natives, make better raw material for television shows.)

1965

Influenced by the vigorous civil rights movement Congress abolished many of the traditional geopolitical discriminations in immigration, adding a new discrimination in favor of *family reunification.* In earlier days when immigration was judged by its effects on labor, priority was given to occupations in which there was asserted to be a domestic shortage of laborers. The new priority given to family members largely negated discrimination in terms of the occupational needs of the receiving country. In making this shift Congress took no note of a basic principle of ecology: the criteria of selection determine the results of an action. After 1965, the admission of a sister could lead to the admission of her husband, and that to the admission of the husband's relations, and so on. Thus a *chain migration* was created, a process that had no foreseeable terminus. In terms of training and proven abilities, many studies have shown that the migrants who came in after 1965 ranked below the immigrants of earlier periods, when family reunification was not a criterion.

"It is a part of primitive human nature to distrust the stranger. There is even a word for this attitude: xenophobia."

1986–1992

Several acts of Congress affected immigration in various ways: in summary, both legal and illegal immigration increased (although the evidence for the second increase is not as firm, of course). Though always controversial, immigration is generally not a popular controversy, perhaps because people have ambivalent feelings about the poor immigrants themselves. Simply put, immigration may be defended as a positive good for either of two reasons: (a) as a benefit to the immigrants; (b) as a benefit to the citizens of the receiving country. Discussants who are most committed to the first goal are—in America—likely to remind their fellow citizens that "we are a nation of immigrants." Under pressure, the idealists may admit that a similar assertion can be made of every nation in the world: it's just that some immigrations are recent while others are very remote. But, say some, is it not selfish of us to deny our land to others? We are expected to be moved by the irony of these anonymous lines:

> We thank Thee Lord that by Thy grace
> Thou brought us to this lovely place.

And now dear Lord we humbly pray
Thou wilt all others keep away.

Emotionally, the argument is a moving one. Its shortcoming is not obvious, but it is nonetheless real: there is no reference in these verses to numbers, either of human beings or of the resources available for human life. It is a literate, or verbal argument; it is not numerate or quantitative.

In the 17th century Galileo said that the great book of the universe is written in mathematical language; the task of scientists—'philosophers', as they were then called—was to show what the numbers mean. In the 20th century Alfred North Whitehead made Galileo's point in even stronger language: "Through and through the world is infected with quantity. To talk sense is to talk in quantities." For three centuries, the natural sciences made magnificent progress following in the footsteps of Galileo and Whitehead. Many now think that certain important non-sciences—ethics, for example—should also take the numerate path.

The Lifeboat

What we should do about immigration is certainly in part an ethical problem. No stable solution is possible so long as we refuse to look at the numbers: the numbers of immigrants; the rates at which they are admitted; the resources available for all the members of an operating group like a nation; and the quantitative consequences of over-stressing the resource base. The "resources of the environment" are subject to constant revision, but at each stage in the development of our thought we must admit that the environment practically available to the human species is limited. The first official recognition of the limitedness of the United States came in a statement made by the Superintendent of the Census that "the unsettled area has been so broken into isolated bodies of settlement that there can hardly be said to be a frontier line." That was said in 1890, though it was some time before most Americans became aware that the frontier was now closed. From 1890 on, citizens looking for space in which to make a living found themselves in increasing competition with other people. It became a matter of national concern whether the increase produced by the natural fertility of the resident population was to be augmented by the admission of more competitors from elsewhere.

"What we should do about immigration is certainly in part an ethical problem."

A metaphor often helps us to get our thoughts straight. Any territory or environment that is admitted to be finite suggests the metaphor of a lifeboat (which is certainly finite). Suppose "this lovely place" referred to in the quatrain above is a lifeboat with a rated capacity of 48 people; and suppose 43 persons are already on board when another supplicant is sighted. And suppose further that we can see another 50 unfortunates swimming toward our boat. Under these conditions, what is the ethical thing to do? Should we take in all the would-be passengers even if the total load far exceeds the prudent estimation of the boat's carrying capacity? Or should we slow down the rate of admission of immigrants as the carrying capacity is approached? Pursuing the first policy will ultimately swamp the boat, producing a disaster for both the original occupants and the newcomers. Pursuing the second policy will confine the disaster to the late-comers. Those who choose the second policy may be called 'heartless', but at least they will not become lifeless.

It may of course be objected that this is only a story, an analogy, a metaphor—not reality itself. But it surely points to the truth of the limitedness of our world. Unfortunately, in the rhetoric of traditional ethics there is almost never any hint of limits. . . .

"Those who think that utterly open borders are a mistake cannot believe that an army of ten million unemployed . . . will not be increased when two million more immigrants are admitted in one year."

There is a danger, of course, in emphasizing any particular limit: one may be wrong. Error may make a decision-maker unnecessarily conservative. Science and technology have, in the past two centuries, pushed aside so many apparent limits that the public has developed a habit of trusting the future to pull the chestnuts of our poor decisions out of the fire. We are urged to "Fly now—Pay later!" But remember: when payday comes around a chronic optimist often finds himself short of the needful.

Misplaced Optimism

It is well to keep in mind the fact that the term *optimism* was coined in 1737 in order to disparage the attitude it stood for. So, in its origins at least, *optimism* shares a birth process with -isms generally. *Optimism* was born under a cloud of mistrust. Will it some day return to its natal condition? An interesting question! The structural optimism of our social system may have been partly responsible for moving immigration out of the Labor department in 1940.

Those whose temperament keeps them from believing in the finiteness of the world find it hard to admit that new immigrants will take jobs from workers already here. By contrast, those who believe in finiteness try to keep the domestic accounts in balance. Those who think that utterly open borders are a mistake cannot believe that an army of ten million unemployed—a typical figure for the U.S.—will not be increased when two million more immigrants are admitted in one year. Controlled immigration becomes the default position of population policy. A heavy burden of proof falls on anyone who proposes doing away with border control.

When it comes to social questions, a single argument is seldom decisive. Above all, we must take the future into account. The present cost of an action may be more than compensated for by future benefits. The promoters of the immigration legislation of 1965 increased the diversity of the incoming stream, an aim that was made fully explicit in the laws of 1990. Within a year Ben Wattenberg, an influential journalist, ecstatically proclaimed that "This is the dawning of the first universal nation. It's going to cause some turmoil, but on balance it's an incredibly poetic fact." Zangwill's melting pot was to be replaced by a salad bowl, an image that was felt to be less condescending and more stable.

This was a remarkable position to take, considering that by this time nations were fissioning right and left throughout the world. In 1989 the Soviet Union dissolved into many semi-autonomous units. Conflict between ethnic groups went on and on in the Holy Land, while murderous 'ethnic cleansing' was used to fragment the highly diverse nation of Yugoslavia. In the light of the observable political fruits of diversity one cannot but question the motives of those who want to increase ethnic diversity within the borders of the United States.

Advocates of Immigration Are Not Hurt by It

The writer Richard Estrada, by birth a member of a minority ethnic group in the U.S., has given a telling criticism of the propaganda for diversity. Replying to Mr. F., another writer, who had urged that we ignore any loss of employment by the laboring class as a result of an open-borders policy, Estrada asked: "Why does Mr. F. not forthrightly advance his open-immigration beliefs by lobbying for the annual importation of, say, three hundred thousand journalists? Perhaps then he could persuade the remaining two of the three professions that are most supportive of massive immigration to lobby for the entry of three hundred thousand economists and three hundred thousand lawyers." (Fact of life: the great majority of legislators were trained to be lawyers.)

Journalists play a key role in generating and nurturing public attitudes. Following the reunion of East and West Germany—the one country poor, the other rich—immigrants started streaming into west German cities, some of which already had an unemployment rate of 40 percent. When young men in the host territory beat up the immigrants, journalists outside Germany confidently labeled the activists "Neo-Nazis" (which they may or may not have been). No doubt the belligerent citizens used scurrilous names for the immigrants (even as American citizens did for their immigrants in earlier days). Obviously the imaginative ability of our safely employed journalists was too feeble to comprehend the grinding reality of competition for scarce jobs. Journalists are clever at inferring motives; they are seldom expert in investigating the logic of a situation.

> ***"Those who make the most propaganda for dismantling the nation through immigration are the ones whose jobs are not in the least threatened by a massive invasion of migrants."***

In evaluating public controversies we would do well to remember a caution often voiced in the sixteenth century by Martin Luther: "It makes a difference whose ox is gored." How often does a demand for open borders come from people who care for the sick, or hand-cultivate vegetables, or put tar on roofs, or dig ditches or wash cars? Essentially never. Those who make the most propaganda for dismantling the nation through immigration are the ones whose jobs are not in the least threatened by a massive invasion of migrants. It is almost impossible for a new immigrant to acquire the skills needed to become a journalist, a lawyer or a university professor in economics. The child of an immigrant may do so years later, after the assimilation process has taken place and an idiomatic mastery of the language has been reached. But new immigrants take jobs only from a restricted body of citizens. It is easy for those who are safely established in their occupations to courageously stand for open borders. It is easy to generously offer the jobs of other people to the would-be immigrants who tug at our heartstrings.

Bibliography

Books

Phillip Anastos and Chris French	*Illegal: Seeking the American Dream*. New York: Rizzoli, 1991.
Brent Ashabranner	*Our Beckoning Borders: Illegal Immigration to America*. New York: Cobblehill Books, 1996.
Roy Beck	*The Case Against Immigration*. New York: W. W. Norton & Company, 1996.
George Borjas	*Heaven's Door*. Princeton, NJ: Princeton University Press, 1999.
Peter Brimelow	*Alien Nation: Common Sense About America's Immigration Disaster*. New York: Random House, 1995.
Wayne A. Cornelius	*Controlling Immigration*. Stanford, CA: Standford University Press, 1994.
Humphrey Dalton, ed.	*Will America Drown? Immigration and the Third World Population Explosion*. Washington, DC: Scott Townsend, 1995.
Venson C. Davis	*Blood on the Border: Criminal Behavior and Illegal Immigration Along the Southern U.S. Border*. New York: Vantage Press, 1993.
Lisa Duran, et al.	*Immigrant Rights—and Wrongs*. Los Angeles: Labor/Community Strategy Center, 1994.
Richard M. Ebeling and Jacob G. Hornberger, eds.	*The Case for Free Trade and Open Immigration*. Washington, DC: Future of Freedom Foundation, 1995.
Todd A. Eisenstadt and Cathryn L. Thorup	*Caring Capacity Versus Carrying Capacity: Community Responses to Mexican Immigration in San Diego's North County*. San Diego: Center for U.S.-Mexican Studies, 1994.
Jonathan L. Fried	*Operation Blockade: A City Divided*. Philadelphia: American Friends Service Committee, 1994.
Scipio Garling and Ira Mehlman	*The Environmentalist's Guide to a Sensible Immigration Policy*. Washington, DC: Federation for American Immigration Reform, 1999.

Georgie Anne Geyer — *Americans No More*. New York: Atlantic Monthly Press, 1997.

David G. Gutierrez, ed. — *Between Two Worlds: Mexican Immigrants in the United States*. Wilmington, DE: SR Books, 1996.

David W. Haines and Karen Elaine Rosenblum, eds. — *Illegal Immigration in America: A Reference Handbook*. New York: Greenwood Publishing Group, 1999.

Garrett Hardin — *The Immigration Dilemma: Avoiding the Tragedy of the Commons*. Washington, DC: Federation for American Immigration Reform, 1995.

William R. Hawkins — *Importing Revolution: Open Borders and the Radical Agenda*. Monterey, VA: American Immigration Control Foundation, 1995.

David M. Heer — *Immigration in America's Future: Social Science Findings and the Policy Debate*. Boulder, CO: Westview Press, 1996.

Robert E. Holmes — *The Criminal Alien*. Sacramento, CA: Senate Publications, 1993.

John Isbister — *The Immigration Debate: Remaking America*. West Hartford, CT: Kumarian Press, 1996.

Hans P. Johnson — *Undocumented Immigration to California*. California: Public Policy Institute of California, 1996.

Peter Kwong — *Forbidden Workers: Illegal Chinese Immigrants and American Labor*. New York: New Press, 1998.

Sarah J. Mahler — *American Dreaming: Immigrant Life on the Margins*. Princeton, NJ: Princeton University Press, 1995.

Nicolaus Mills and Toni Morrison, eds. — *Arguing Immigration: The Debate over the Changing Face of America*. New York: Simon & Schuster, 1994.

Jeanne Schinto — *Huddle Fever: Living in the Immigrant City*. New York: Knopf, 1995.

Julian L. Simon — *Immigration: The Demographic and Economic Facts*. Washington, DC: Cato Institute/National Immigration Forum, 1995.

Sanford J. Ungar — *Fresh Blood: The New American Immigrants*. New York: Simon & Schuster, 1995.

Phil Williams, ed. — *Illegal Immigration and Commercial Sex: The New Slave Trade*. New York: Frank & Cass, 1999.

Periodicals

Trevor Armbrister — "Our Drug-Plagued Mexican Border," *Reader's Digest*, January 1996.

Ray Borane — "Do You Hire Illegal Immigrants?" *New York Times*, August 30, 1999.

George J. Borjas	"The New Economics of Immigration," *Atlantic Monthly*, November 1996.
Michael Finkel	"Desperate Passage," *New York Times Magazine*, June 18, 2000.
Samuel Francis	"Immigrants Have No Plans to Assimilate," *Conservative Chronicle*, June 14, 2000. Available from PO Box 11297, Des Moines, IA 50340-1297.
Samuel Francis	"Open Borders Cost American Lives," *Conservative Chronicle*, September 3, 1997.
Daniel Golden	"No Green Card Means American Education Is a Win-Lose Prospect," *Wall Street Journal*, June 22, 2000.
Donald L. Huddle	"Immigrants, Jobs, and Wages: The Misuses of Econometrics," *NPG Forum*, April 1992. Available from Negative Population Growth, Inc., PO Box 1206, Teaneck, NJ 07666.
Matthew Jardine	"Operation Gatekeeper," *Peace Review*, September 1998.
Nancie L. Katz	"Groups Blast US Treatment of Illegal Immigrants," *Christian Science Monitor*, April 10, 1997.
Howard LaFranchi	"America Puts Up Chain-Links Along a Once-Friendly Border," *Christian Science Monitor*, February 13, 1996.
Howard LaFranchi	"US-Bound Migrants Find Town In Guatemala No Haven," *Christian Science Monitor*, June 25, 1996.
Charles Levendosky	"Slam the Door on Secret Evidence," *Progressive Populist*, July 1, 2000.
Anthony Lewis	"Mean and Petty," *New York Times*, April 12, 1996.
Norman Matloff	"How Immigration Harms Minorities," *Public Interest*, Summer 1996.
Scott McConnell	"Americans No More?" *National Review*, December 31, 1997.
Patrick J. McDonnell	"Illegal Immigrant Population in U.S. Now Tops 5 Million," *Los Angeles Times*, February 8, 1997. Available from Times Mirror Square, Los Angeles, CA 90053.
Tim McGirk	"Border Clash," *Time*, June 26, 2000.
Bill McKibben	"Immigrants Aren't the Problem. We Are," *New York Times*, March 9, 1998.
Joel Millman and Marjorie Valbrun	"Arizona Towns Thrive As 'Border Jumpers' Come and Go," *Wall Street Journal*, May 26, 1999.
Mary Anastasia O'Grady	"Mr. President, Tear Down This Wall," *Wall Street Journal*, October 3, 1997.
Frank del Olmo	"End Border Hysteria and Move On," *Los Angeles Times*, September 14, 1997.

José Palafox — "Militarizing the Border," *Covert Action Quarterly*, Spring 1996.

Richard Rodriguez — "An Ideal of America Is Clubbed," *Los Angeles Times*, April 7, 1996.

Jeffrey Rosen — "Good Help," *New Republic*, February 15, 1993.

Eric Schmitt — "Illegal Immigrants Rose to 5 Million in '96," *New York Times*, February 8, 1997.

Emanuel Sferios — "Population, Immigration, and the Environment," *Z Magazine*, June 1998.

Julian L. Simon, et al. — "Why Control the Borders?" *National Review*, February 1, 1993.

Deborah Sontag — "Poor and Deaf Mexicans, Betrayed in Their Hope," *New York Times*, July 25, 1997.

Dan Stein — "Born in the USA—But Not American," *Christian Science Monitor*, October 25, 1996.

Daniel W. Sutherland — "Identity Crisis," *Reason*, December 1997.

Marjorie Valbrun — "At the Frontier of Irony, Border Patrol's Ranks Swell with Hispanics," *Wall Street Journal*, October 22, 1998.

Village Voice — "Alien Nation," February 2, 1993. Available from 36 Cooper Square, New York, NY 10003.

Tim Weiner — "Pleas for Asylum Inundate System for Immigration," *New York Times*, April 25, 1993.

Organizations to Contact

The editors have compiled the following list of organizations that are concerned with the issues debated in this book. All of them have publications or information available for interested readers. The descriptions are derived from materials provided by the organizations. This list was compiled at the date of publication. Names, addresses, and phone numbers of organizations are subject to change.

American Civil Liberties Union (ACLU)
132 W. 43d St., New York, NY 10036
(212) 944-9800 • fax: (212) 921-7916
website: www.aclu.org/

The ACLU is a national organization that champions the rights found in the Declaration of Independence and the U.S. Constitution. The ACLU Immigrants' Rights Project works with refugees and immigrants facing deportation, and with immigrants in the workplace. It has published reports, position papers, and a book, *The Rights of Aliens and Refugees*, that detail what freedoms immigrants and refugees have under the U.S. Constitution.

American Friends Service Committee (AFSC)
1501 Cherry St., Philadelphia, PA 19102
(215) 241-7000 • fax: (215) 241-7275
e-mail: afscinfo@afsc.org • website: www.afsc.org

The AFSC is a Quaker organization that attempts to relieve human suffering and find new approaches to world peace and social justice through nonviolence. It lobbies against what it believes to be unfair immigration laws, especially criminalizing the employment of illegal immigrants. It has published *Sealing Our Borders: The Human Toll*, a report documenting human rights violations committed by law enforcement agents against immigrants.

American Immigration Control Foundation (AICF)
PO Box 525, Monterey, VA 24465
(703) 468-2022 • fax: (703) 468-2024

AICF is an independent research and education organization that believes massive immigration, especially illegal immigration, is harming America. It calls for an end to illegal immigration and for stricter controls on legal immigration. The foundation publishes the monthly newsletter *Border Watch* and two pamphlets: John Vinson's *Immigration Out of Control*, and Lawrence Auster's *The Path to National Suicide: An Essay on Immigration and Multiculturalism.*

American Immigration Lawyers Association (AILA)
1400 I St. NW, Suite 1200, Washington, DC 20005
(202) 216-2400 • fax: (202) 371-9449
website: www.aila.org/

AILA is a professional association of lawyers who work in the field of immigration and nationality law. It publishes the *AILA Immigration Journal* and compiles and distributes a continuously updated bibliography of government and private documents on immigration laws and regulations.

Americans for Immigration Control (AIC)
725 Second St. NE, Suite 307, Washington, DC 20002
(202) 543-3719 • fax: (202) 543-5811

AIC is a lobbying organization that works to influence Congress to adopt legal reforms that would reduce U.S. immigration. It calls for increased funding for the U.S. Border Patrol and the deployment of military forces to prevent illegal immigration. It also supports sanctions against employers who hire illegal immigrants and opposes amnesty for such immigrants. AIC offers articles and brochures that state its position on immigration.

Americas Watch (AW)
485 Fifth Ave., New York, NY 10017
(212) 972-8400 • fax: (212) 972-0905

AW, a division of Human Rights Watch, is an organization that promotes human rights, especially for Latin Americans. It publicizes human rights violations and encourages international protests against governments responsible for them. AW has published *Brutality Unchecked: Human Rights Abuses Along the U.S. Border with Mexico.*

The Brookings Institution
1775 Massachusetts Ave. NW, Washington, DC 20036-2188
(202) 797-6104 • fax: (202) 797-6319
e-mail: brookinfo@brook.edu • website: www.brook.edu

The institution, founded in 1927, is a liberal research and education organization that publishes material on economics, government, and foreign policy. It publishes analyses of immigration issues in its quarterly journal, *Brookings Review*, and in various books and reports.

California Coalition for Immigration Reform (CCIR)
PO Box 2744-117, Huntington Beach, CA 92649
(714) 665-2500 • fax: (714) 846-9682
website: www.ccir.net

CCIR is a grassroots volunteer organization representing Americans concerned with illegal immigration. It seeks to educate and inform the public and to effectively ensure enforcement of the nation's immigration laws. CCIR publishes alerts, bulletins, and the monthly newsletter *911*.

Cato Institute
1000 Massachusetts Ave. NW, Washington, DC 20001-5403
(202) 842-0200 • fax: (202) 842-3490
website: www.cato.org

The institute is a libertarian public policy research foundation dedicated to stimulating policy debate. It believes immigration is good for the U.S. economy and favors easing immigration restrictions. As well as various articles on immigration, the institute has published the book *The Economic Consequences of Immigration* by Julian L. Simon.

Center for Immigrants Rights (CIR)
48 St. Mark's Pl., 4th Fl, New York, NY 10003
(212) 505-6890

The center offers immigrants information concerning their rights. It provides legal support, advocacy, and assistance to immigrants and strives to influence immigration policy. The center publishes fact sheets on immigrant rights and immigration law and the quarterly newsletter *CIR Report*.

Center for Immigration Studies
1522 K St. NW, Suite 820, Washington, DC 20005-1202
(202) 466-8185 • fax: (202) 466-8076
e-mail: center@cis.org • website: www.cis.org

The center studies the effects of immigration on the economic, social, demographic, and environmental conditions in the United States. It believes that the large number of recent immigrants has become a burden on America and favors reforming immigration laws to make them consistent with U.S. interests. The center publishes reports, position papers, and the quarterly journal *Scope*.

El Rescate
2675 W. Olympic Blvd., Los Angeles, CA 90006
(213) 387-3284

El Rescate provides free legal and social services to Central American refugees. It is involved in federal litigation to uphold the constitutional rights of refugees and illegal immigrants. It compiles and distributes articles and information and publishes the newsletter *El Rescate*.

Federation for American Immigration Reform (FAIR)
1666 Connecticut Ave. NW, Suite 400, Washington, DC 20009
(202) 328-7004 • fax: (202) 387-3447
e-mail: info@fairus.org • website: www.fairus.org

FAIR works to stop illegal immigration and to limit legal immigration. It believes that the growing flood of immigrants into the United States causes higher unemployment and taxes social services. FAIR has published many reports and position papers, including *Ten Steps to Securing America's Borders* and *Immigration 2000: The Century of the New American Sweatshop*.

Foundation for Economic Education, Inc. (FEE)
30 S. Broadway, Irvington, NY 10533
(914) 591-7230 • fax: (914) 591-8910
e-mail: fee@fee.org • website: www.fee.org/

FEE publishes information and research in support of capitalism, free trade, and limited government. It occasionally publishes articles opposing government restrictions on immigration in its monthly magazine *The Freeman*.

The Heritage Foundation
214 Massachusetts Ave. NE, Washington, DC 20002-4999
(202) 546-4400 • fax: (202) 546-8328
e-mail: info@heritage.org • website: www.heritage.org/

The foundation is a conservative public policy research institute. It has published articles pertaining to immigration in its Backgrounder series and in its quarterly journal *Policy Review*.

National Alliance Against Racist and Political Repression (NAARPR)
11 John St., Rm. 702, New York, NY 10038
(212) 406-3330 • fax: (212) 406-3542

NAARPR is a coalition of political, labor, church, civic, student, and community organizations that oppose the many forms of human rights repression in the United States. It seeks to end the harassment and deportation of illegal immigrant workers. The alliance publishes pamphlets and a quarterly newsletter *The Organizer*.

National Coalition of Advocates for Students (NCAS)
100 Boylston St., Suite 737, Boston, MA 02116-4610
(617) 357-8507• fax: (617) 357-9549
e-mail: ncasmfe@mindspring.com • website: www.ncas1.org/

NCAS is a national network of child advocacy organizations that work on public school issues. Through its Immigrant Student Program it works to ensure that immigrants are given sufficient and appropriate education. The coalition has published two book-length reports: *New Voices: Immigrant Students in U.S. Public Schools* and *Immigrant Students: Their Legal Right of Access to Public Schools*.

National Council of La Raza (NCLR)
1111 19th St. NW, Suite 1000, Washington, DC 20036
(202) 289-1380 • fax: (202) 289-8173
website: www.nclr.org/

NCLR is a national organization that seeks to improve opportunities for Americans of Hispanic descent. It conducts research on many issues, including immigration, and opposes restrictive immigration laws. The council publishes and distributes congressional testimony and reports, including *Unfinished Business: The Immigration Control and Reform Act of 1986* and *Unlocking the Golden Door: Hispanics and the Citizenship Process*.

National Immigration Forum
220 I St. NE, Suite 220, Washington, DC 20002-4362
(202) 544-0004 • fax: (202) 544-1905
website: www.immigrationforum.org

The forum believes that legal immigrants strengthen America and that welfare benefits do not attract illegal immigrants. It supports effective measures aimed at curbing illegal immigration and promotes programs and policies that help refugees and immigrants assimilate into American society. The forum publishes the quarterly newsletter *The Golden Door* and the bimonthly newsletter *Immigration Policy Matters*.

The National Network for Immigrant and Refugee Rights
310 Eighth St., Suite 307, Oakland, CA 94607
(510) 465-1984 • fax: (510) 465-1885
website: www.nnirr.org/frame.html

The network includes community, church, labor, and legal groups committed to the cause of equal rights for all immigrants. These groups work to end discrimination and unfair treatment of illegal immigrants and refugees. The network aims to strengthen and coordinate educational efforts among immigration advocates nationwide. It publishes a monthly newsletter *Network News*.

Negative Population Growth, Inc. (NPG)
1717 Massachusetts Ave. NW, Suite 101, Washington, DC 20036
(202) 667-8950 • fax: (202) 667-8953
e-mail: npg@npg.org • website: www.npg.org

NPG believes that world population must be reduced and that the United States is already overpopulated. It calls for an end to illegal immigration and an annual cap on legal immigration of 200,000 people. This would achieve "zero net migration" because

200,000 people exit the country each year, according to NPG. NPG frequently publishes position papers on population and immigration in its *NPG Forum*.

The Rockford Institute
928 N. Main St., Rockford, IL 61103-7061
(815) 964-5053 • fax: (815) 965-1827
e-mail: info@rockfordinstitute.org • website: www.rockfordinstitute.org/

The institute is a conservative research center that studies capitalism, religion, and liberty. It has published numerous articles questioning immigration and legalization policies in its monthly magazine *Chronicles*.

United States General Accounting Office (GAO)
441 G St. NW, Washington, DC 20548
(202) 275-2812
website: www.gao.gov

The GAO is the investigative arm of the U.S. Congress and is charged with examining all matters related to the receipt and disbursement of public funds. It frequently publishes reports evaluating the effectiveness of U.S. immigration policies.

Voice of Citizens Together (VCT)
13547 Ventura Blvd., Suite 163, Sherman Oaks, CA 92423
(818) 501-2061 • fax: (818) 501-0359
website: www.instanet.com/~vct

VCT is a grassroots organization that collects and disseminates information on immigration. Its members believe that uncontrolled immigration presents a threat to the community, economy, and culture of the United States. VCT publishes a monthly newsletter that presents its findings on immigration.

Index